GEORGETTE HEYER'S
REGENCY ENGLAND

DEDICATION

To Susan Edwards for introducing me to Georgette
Heyer, and sharing twenty years of reading pleasure.

And to George Thomas Simons, my father, for manfully
taking on the novels and enjoying 'her world'.

*The publishers wish to thank
Jonathan Potter Limited, 21 Grosvenor Street,
London W1X 9FE and The Map House,
54 Beauchamp Place, London SW3 1NY
for the use of the maps in this book.*

First published in Great Britain in 1989
by Sidgwick & Jackson Limited
1 Tavistock Chambers, Bloomsbury Way
London WC1A 2SG

ISBN 0 283 99832 6

Photoset by Rowland Phototypesetting Limited
Bury St Edmunds, Suffolk
Printed in Great Britain by
The Bath Press Limited, Bath

GEORGETTE HEYER'S
REGENCY ENGLAND

Teresa Chris

Illustrations by
Arthur Barbosa

Sidgwick & Jackson
London

CONTENTS

◆

INTRODUCTION

◆

*F*or more than fifty years, millions of readers worldwide have enjoyed the Regency romances of Georgette Heyer. Her audience continues to grow with each generation as her fans, old and new, reread the novels, appreciating the sheer elegance and wit of her prose style, and relating to the wonderfully vivid characters who stay alive to us long after the last page is turned.

Georgette Heyer created her own special Regency world based on an exact knowledge of the period. We, the readers, can escape completely into this world, as she vividly conjures up the mores of the time, the preoccupations of the people, the language in which they conversed, and the niceties of their social intercourse. It is a world which is fascinating to us, even today, because such a severe order was imposed and everybody knew their place. The 'ton' set the standard; from the select dances at Almacks to the propriety of racing down to Brighton in a curricle. The term 'the ton', from the French word meaning everything that is fashionable, had come into usage in England in the latter half of the eighteenth century and by the Regency period it denoted the cream of society. Georgette Heyer's appealing characters are bound by the conventions of this world but more often delight us by rebelling against it.

Georgette Heyer died in 1974, so there is a finite number of her Regency romances that we can enjoy; we are, in fact, lucky to have as many as we do. She was an extremely private, if prolific, person and didn't, outside her books, spend much time commenting on the world she had created. Of the over fifty novels which Georgette Heyer wrote, twenty-four are set in the Regency period. She was a stickler for accuracy and compiled copious notebooks full of details of Regency life, including drawings of items of dress and the different carriages used in the period. She meticulously researched her facts, and knew, for example, every turnpike on the Great North Road. The odd, but memorable, expressions her characters use were culled from her extensive reading and jotted down for future use.

The contemporary detail enhances the credibility of the novels and increases our pleasure in them, but it is the characters who give the novels the unique life which makes her readers lifelong fans. Georgette Heyer's heroines are often young and spirited, appealing in their inventiveness, and for falling into social scrapes from which they constantly need to be rescued. In the later novels however, a new maturity is seen. The heroines are older and wiser, 'no longer in their first bloom', often financially independent. They confront the hero on a more equal footing and the relationships which develop are surprisingly akin to those that men and women experience today. Georgette Heyer brings them all convincingly to life but unfortunately these characters live only between the covers of each book.

There is however one element in her books that is real and still exists for us today and that is the settings where her characters fell in love, strolled to the library, met the Prince Regent, sheltered from the rain, or fought their duels. London, Brighton, Bath and other locations all around England are rich in Regency heritage and hence rich in memories for fans who can recall each nuance of their heroines' romances or adventures. This book will explore the settings of that world so that the reader may once again enjoy parts of the novels in the places where they actually happened.

So often, whilst in the street, by raising the eyes above the modern frontages and switching our perception, we can plunge ourselves into Georgette Heyer's Regency England, and experience her world anew. In some places, like Bath, it is even possible to have afternoon tea and to listen to a quartet in the Pump Room while remembering how Abby who was 'neither in her first bloom' nor 'an accredited beauty' agreed to take a stroll about the room with Miles Calverleigh, the *Black Sheep* of the title, allowing herself to be beguiled by his iconoclastic remarks and droll wit.

Whilst many of the settings are still the same as they were over one hundred and fifty years ago, it is, in some cases, only a name that will connect us with a familiar scene. Where possible a number of gentle walking tours have been included in this book, pointing out the Regency landmarks mentioned in the novels, and recalling the most romantic, exciting or funny scenes that happened there.

Georgette Heyer's Regency England will give pleasure to anyone who has read Georgette Heyer's work and wanted more.

CHAPTER I

MALE PRESERVES:
The St James's Area

Piccadilly Circus is a central point from which an exploration of the St James's area of Georgette Heyer's London may begin. Walk south down Regent Street until it becomes Waterloo Place. As you travel, you will find that you leave much of the bustle of modern-day London behind, retreating into the elegant streets of Regency London. One of the major joys of following in the footsteps of Georgette Heyer's characters is that we see parts of London that we might never have thought of visiting. Before continuing down to the monument dominating the far ground, pause in the middle of the road at Pall Mall. This is where the much-mentioned Carlton House once stood. Carlton House was the London home of the Prince Regent and gave its name to the famous, or infamous, depending on your point of view, Carlton House set. Where you now stand was once the centre of the fashionable world, and the Prince Regent, with little regard to expense, spent many happy years constantly redecorating the interior of Carlton House and entertaining lavishly. At the Prince's balls the coaches carrying the guests would stretch in a line all the way to the top of Bond Street, inching slowly forward to deliver their elaborately dressed occupants. When the Prince Regent became King, however, he moved to Buckingham Palace. Carlton House was demolished in 1826.

Mr Chawleigh, Jenny's city-bred father in *A Civil Contract*, was thrilled when Jenny told him that she had met the Prince Regent who was both very civil to Adam and herself, and expressed the hope that he would 'see them at Carlton House one day'. Not long after, there arrived a gilt-edged card inviting them to

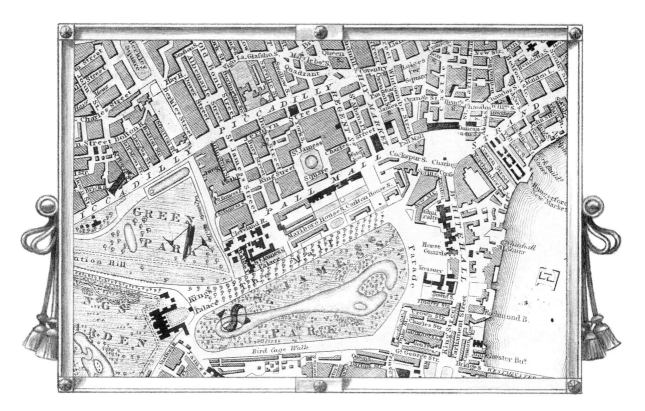

Carlton House to meet Her Majesty the Queen at a dress party. This invitation put all others into the shade as far as Jenny was concerned, and despite the fact that she was pregnant and not feeling very well, she refused to leave London because she didn't want to miss the auspicious event. Mr Chawleigh was 'dazzled by a vision of vicarious grandeur' and, gleefully rubbing his hands together, constantly reread the invitation aloud during visits to his daughter's house. When Jenny finally attended the fête at Carlton House, she was somewhat disappointed to see no more of the House than its Great Hall. Apparently this had a 'coved ceiling and yellow porphyry pillars'. An enormous polygon room had been created by Nash in the garden, and this 'was hung with white muslin, with mirrors past counting flinging back the lights of hundreds of candles'. Jenny felt she had never before seen anything so beautiful.

Arabella, in the novel of the same name, was also very excited by her gilt-edged invitation to a Dress Party at Carlton House. Mr Beaumaris, however, thought that the Regent's parties were dreadful 'squeezes' and subject to 'such vulgarities as a fountain playing in the middle of the dinner-table'! Arabella, who had not yet adopted the attitude of being blasé or bored by everything in the metropolis, exclaimed with delight at her first dress party at Carlton House. She was so impressed that she momentarily forgot the awkwardness that existed between Mr Beaumaris and herself as she gazed at the enormous 'cut-glass chandelier, reflected, with its myriad of candles, in four large pier-glasses'. Mr Beaumaris took her to see the Conservatory, which Arabella found to be more like a very ugly cathedral. The statue of Venus Asleep was housed there, and they were bemused to find that, for some inexplicable reason, it was covered in a veil of light gauze.

Leaving the site of Carlton House, walk on down Waterloo Place to the tall obelisk in front of you. It is a memorial to Frederick, Duke of York, who lived from 1763 until 1827, and was the second son of George III. Fact blends with fiction here as he is mentioned in several of the novels. When Judith Taverner, in *Regency Buck*, received a 'very gratifying invitation' to stay at Belvoir Castle, she found that the Duke of York was the most notable guest there. According to custom he always had the same suite of rooms when he stayed at Belvoir. Lord Ombersley, in *The Grand Sophy*, brought the Duke to the highly successful dress ball that Sophy had orchestrated at the Ombersley house. Like all the royal princes the Duke of York was immensely fat and 'in imminent danger of bursting out of his tightly stretched pantaloons.' He was another 'genial prince', however, and chatted happily with the guests until he withdrew to the library for a rubber of whist. Known as the 'Grand Old Duke of York' it was he whose reputation suffered in the army scandal concerning 'perks' for promotions.

Standing at the memorial is like being at the top of a short cliff. On either side stretches the classical Carlton Terrace; when built, it was the most exclusive and sought after address in London, and below, in season, is a sea of green – the green of St James's Park. It is hard to ignore the heavy preponderance of traffic rolling by and to remember instead the park filled with the 'barques of frailty' who made it their parading ground, their phaetons and other carriages stylishly driving up and down, displaying their owners' wares.

Go down the steps and look along at the impressive vista the terrace presents; then walk to your right. If you are lucky you might see a troop of horseguards going by, which will really give you a feeling of what it must have been like to see the parks full of people on horseback, especially such fine specimens. The clop of their hooves and jingle of the harness *en masse* are sounds from another era. You will shortly come to a set of forked steps leading up to an oval driveway. From the balustrade at the top of the steps there is a fine view over St James's Park.

Carlton Gardens is up a little way on your left; turn into it and walk up to Pall Mall. Pall Mall used to be one of the main roads into London. As Mr Kit Fancot travelled into town in *False Colours*, he noticed that the old oil-burners along here had been replaced by gas-lighting, which had been installed by private enterprise in 1807 and was soon to light up the rest of central London. Pall Mall was notorious in the Regency period for housing 'certain establishments' most notable for gaming. Evelyn Fancot, the more disreputable of the two twins, contracted disastrous gaming debts when he was lured into some 'Pall Mall hell' when fresh upon the town. And Sir Waldo, in *The Nonesuch*, had financially rescued Laurence Calver when he was 'bit at that hell in Pall Mall'. Hubert, in *The Grand Sophy*, was foolhardy enough to visit such a place and sustained such losses that he was forced to pledge a family ring at the money lender's, which Sophy retrieved for him at gun-point. A 'discreet house' here in Pall Mall was also instrumental in temporarily ruining Bertram in *Arabella*. While the first evening proved him to be lucky, the second night he came away a 'substantial loser', plunging him into the disastrous care of Leaky Peg.

Walk down Pall Mall past all the famous men's clubs until you reach St James's Palace, which is just past Marlborough House. In the Palace is the Chapel Royal, which was the most fashionable place for the characters in the novels to worship. You can still attend services at the Chapel on Sundays. The royal personages who came here provided a constant draw for the rest of the status conscious 'ton'. Needless to say, not everyone came in pursuit of religion. Judith Taverner and Mrs Scattergood in *Regency Buck* attended morning service here. While Judith tried to keep her mind on the ecclesiastical element, Mrs Scattergood was busy observing the latest fashions. Judith was, however, amused to hear the Duke of Cambridge talking out loud to himself and responding to the dictates of the lesson. Apparently he had no intention of obeying the Bible's behest by giving half his goods to the poor! In fact, Mrs Scattergood informed Judith that the Duke was on the lookout for a rich wife. Outside, after the service, the Duke of Clarence, 'a burly, red-faced gentleman with very staring blue eyes and a pear-shaped head', begged his companion to introduce him to Miss Taverner. Like his brothers, he always had an eye for a pretty woman – especially one who was also wealthy.

Nell, in *April Lady*, normally attended the Chapel Royal, but on one particular occasion her elaborate toilette was so interrupted by the tantrums of Letty and the subsequent discussion with Cardross about what to do with her, that she was very late and decided to go to the Grosvenor Chapel instead, which, as

St James, London

◆

Georgette Heyer so pointedly tells her readers, was 'hardly worthy' of Nell's dresser's 'best efforts'.

In *Arabella*, the heroine, whose father was a vicar, was worried that her hostess, Lady Bridlington, might not attend church on Sunday. However, Lady

Bridlington was meticulous in her observances and often decided to go to the Chapel Royal where not only could she hear a good sermon, but also see 'her more distinguished friends, and even, very often, some member of the Royal Family'. Arabella was lucky (so she told her brothers and sisters at home in the vicarage), to meet the Duke of Clarence, who is kind enough to compliment her on her pink hat, which her Mama had made for her. Arabella did not dare include in her letter the information that the Duke of Clarence 'talked quite audibly in church', as she knew that would not please the family at home.

Go back out of Friary Court and turn to your left. Virtually opposite to St James's Palace is St James's Street – its long sweep heading up the hill to Piccadilly. Beware, ladies, as you stroll up here and into the rest of the St James's area. As Georgette Heyer noted in *April Lady*, this part of London 'belonged almost exclusively to the Gentlemen, and it was not considered good ton for a lady to be seen within its bounds'. St James's Street housed the most famous clubs of the day, and the surrounding streets were full of 'bachelor lodgings and gaming hells'.

Enough of the original buildings have survived to create an authentic backdrop for the Regency characters and bustling life that thronged this street. The first notable building on your right is the very old shop front of Berry Bros and Rudd Ltd – don't fail to notice the sign hanging over the front. At the weekend or in the evening old shutters cover the windows but during opening hours you can see the unique interior of this select and unaltered shop. Next to it is a narrow alleyway, totally unspoilt, that leads to Pickering Place. Here, more than anywhere else in London, it is possible to imagine oneself in another era. Go through the alleyway – taking in the old wood panelling and the flagstones underfoot – into the tiny courtyard. Notice also the old, large hanging lamps. At Number five lived Lady Hamilton – Lord Nelson's mistress. In this quiet cul-de-sac was a 'new gaming hell' to which Revesby introduced Lord Sheringham, in the hope of changing his luck in *Friday's Child*. Sherry was amazed by the outward discreet air of the house, and the way they were inspected by a man through an 'iron grille in the door' before being allowed to enter. Unfortunately the visit was not a success for Sherry, even though he played the card game macao until dawn. Number five was named in *Regency Buck* as a 'hell', and Judith Taverner was very much concerned that her young brother Peregrine had begun to frequent such places. Lord Gaywood, whom Georgette Heyer described as a 'great rattle' tried to liven up the Duke of Sale's life in *The Foundling* by inviting him to a gambling den in Pickering Place, assuring him that the play was very fair!

Tempting though it is to stay in this tranquil by-water of the past, go back onto St James's Street. Don't forget to look at Lock and Co., the hatters, with their selection of old top hats; and Lobb and Lobb the bootmakers, as surviving examples of Regency shops. Lock's made all their hats to measure: from the black top hats worn by the dandies in town to the chapeau bras which were an essential part of a gentleman's evening wear. Continue walking up St James's Street until you reach Ryder Street on your right.

On Ryder Street was the famous Nonesuch Club. Mr Beaumaris, the urbane hero of *Arabella*, was unfortunately holding the bank there the evening that Bertram decided to accept Lord Wivenhoe's invitation to risk his last twenty guineas at the faro tables. Faced with the choice of irrevocably snubbing the young man and knowingly letting him play with his last few pounds, Beaumaris was faced with a tremendous social dilemma, unhelped by Lord Fetersham, who was dreaming of tea! As was so often the case with desperate people, Bertram's play was not successful, and he left, to his horror, six hundred pounds in debt.

Ryder Street is also where Nell Cardross in *April Lady* journeyed, hoping to find the lodging place of Mr Allandale – after being told that Letty had gone there armed with the necessities for a flight to the border. Driving in a hack, and seeing the lighted windows of the clubs as she passed along St James's, Nell was very conscious of the impropriety of her being here. Not only that, but she didn't know the number of Allandale's house. Luckily she recalled that Mr Hethersett lived on the same street and, much to his social embarrassment, she approached him for help. It is not hard to imagine them standing here in the dark evening light: Mr Hethersett in his knee-breeches and silk stockings, waistcoat and swallow-tailed coat, arguing about the propriety of Nell arriving in a common hack and asking for Allandale's direction. It wasn't until the lamplighter arrived with his ladder, and Nell had become very tired of standing in the street, that Felix disclosed the fact that they had been standing outside Allandale's lodging the whole time!

It was on the corner of Ryder Street and St James's that Dysart and Mr Wittering of *April Lady* argued – in their very inebriated state – about the chances of success for Wellington in the coming year. Mr Hethersett patiently waited while Dysart illustrated his points with diagrams on the pavement, impressed by Dysart's knowledge and surprised at how seriously the supposed dilettante was taking the subject.

Pickering Place, London

◆

Finally, one of Georgette Heyer's most appealing, yet less obvious heroes, Freddy Standen, in *Cotillion*, also lived on Ryder Street.

Just before you reach the chemist, which was first opened in 1790, you will see an elegant white building on your right. This houses the famous club, Boodles. Although it is actually number 28, it doesn't advertise this fact. Externally, it hasn't changed since the early nineteenth century. As long as the shutters are

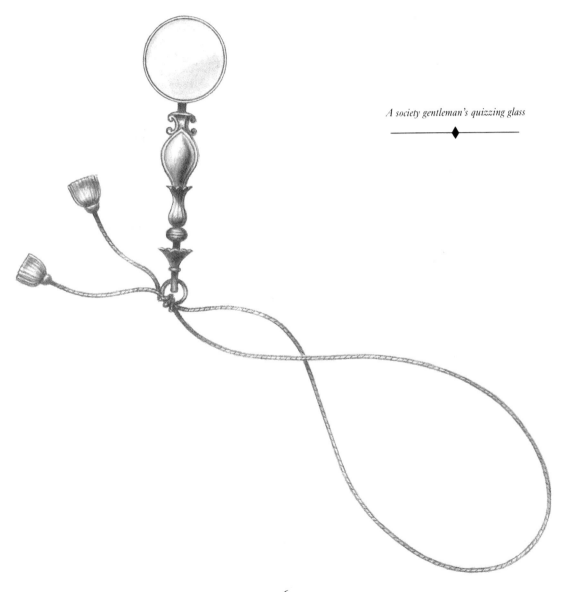

A society gentleman's quizzing glass

not drawn, you can see inside quite well. The club has one of the famous bow windows, in which the dandies and other gentlemen used to sit to quiz the passersby. One of the most respectable clubs to be patronized by the 'ton', this was where Jack Westruther, the most rakish and dashing of the cousins in *Cotillion*, met Biddenden. Jack, who was already sufficiently piqued by Kitty Charing's engagement to Freddy, was *now* told that she was likely to marry the slow-witted Dolphinton before the year was out. Their discussion became so heated that Lord Biddenden was tempted to punch Westruther. But, as Jack reminded him, 'Your credit would never survive a vulgar brawl in Boodles'.

In *Arabella*, Mr Beaumaris, who was concerned about what had happened to Bertram – whom he left in debt in London – decided to track him down through Bertram's friend Mr Scunthorpe. Being told that Mr Scunthorpe was on his way to Boodles, he headed towards St James's Street and successfully accosted his man there.

Across the road from Boodles, in the brick building with the iron railings in front, is the perhaps even more famous Brooks's Club. While peeking in the windows to catch a glimpse of this old-world bastion of masculinity, don't forget to note the old lead flower pots in front. Adam, in *A Civil Contract*, was a member of Brooks's, and it was here that he repaired after persuading his man of business, Wimmering, to buy up all the stock he could, in the belief that Wellington would triumph in the engagement against Napoleon. He dined at the club but was afterwards irritated by the conversation of the pessimists who said that the battle was already lost. Finally, not able to find peace anywhere in the club, he retired to his hotel. The news had been so bad that by the time Adam returned to the club the next evening, he was convinced that his gamble had been hopeless and all his dreams of restoring the fortunes of Fontley and his land were crushed. A large group of men led by Lord Grey were in the very room that lies in front of us overlooking St James's, discussing vociferously the latest developments, when suddenly they heard cheering in the street. Adam peered out of the window into the dusk and saw a chaise with 'Eagles' sticking out of the window. As Georgette Heyer says, 'Pandemonium broke out', with strangers clapping one another on the back, and even the 'most rabid opponents of the war huzza-ed'. Adam, suffering from reaction, felt sick and giddy as the champagne was popped open all around him.

The last club you should take a look at as you continue up St James's is White's, which is the second to last building on the right before you reach Piccadilly. This again has a bow window, but also boasts the original lamps outside, some impressive boot-scrapers, and a wrought-iron balcony. The famous four of the Bow-window set could be seen here, ensconced in the window. Mr Brummell had decreed that they should not 'acknowledge salutations from acquaintances in the street if they were seated in the club window'. Lord Worth, in *Regency Buck* was a member of the Bow-window set but not of the unique four which consisted of 'your complete dandies – Brummell, Alvanley, Mildmay and Pierrepoint'.

This was also one of *the* clubs to belong to. Peregrine in *Regency Buck* asked his guardian, Worth, if he could have him made a member. In *April Lady*, Lord Penvensey – as part of launching his son Dysart into society – introduced him to this club. Sherry was disgusted to hear his wife Hero's projected race against Lady Royston being discussed at the club in the novel *Friday's Child*.

Lord Bridlington in *Arabella* felt it his duty to inform his mother that bets were being made in White's for and against Miss Tallant being able to resist the advances of Mr Beaumaris. He believed, however, that the gentleman's attentions sprung not so much from a sincere affection for Arabella, but more from the pique of being rebuffed – an experience with which Mr Beaumaris was not familiar.

Fenton's Hotel was on the west side of this street, and that was where Sherry and Hero stayed when they were first married. Adam, in *A Civil Contract*, also patronized Fenton's Hotel and found it convenient to walk to Brooks's from there. Before he was married, Sherry, like many of the male characters, had lived in lodgings off St James's Street, but these were definitely not suitable to bring a bride back to.

Having now sallied up this street with impunity, gaze back down it and remember the strictures of the Regency period. St James's would have been populated by the Corinthians, the dandies, the Pink of the Ton, the Fribbles – beaver hats, curly brims, curricles of every description – but no lady of 'ton' in sight.

One of the first things that Judith Taverner learned upon coming to London was that no woman would be seen walking or driving down St James's Street. Arabella, in her letter home to the vicarage, mentioned that it was 'very fast' to be seen walking down this street. Hero, in *Friday's Child*, was always getting into scrapes because she had no idea of what was done and not done, and she unwittingly drove down St James's Street in her phaeton while her husband Sherry was away.

The most amusing scene to recall as you look down St James's Street is one

The Boodles Club, London

from *The Grand Sophy*. Sophy must be Georgette Heyer's most outrageous heroine. Used to being her own mistress and mixing in exalted and very cosmopolitan company, she also had a strong sense of humour. No one ever got the better of Sophy. The prim, censorious Miss Wraxton, who was overly conscious of her own dignity and self-worth, misguidedly tried to direct Sophy's conduct. She goaded Sophy by saying that her own 'character is sufficiently well-established to do . . . what others might be imprudent to attempt'. The devil in Sophy prompted her to test this by immediately driving Miss Wraxton down the length of St James's Street in her dashing phaeton. Nothing could have shocked the prudish lady more, and it is amusing to think of her trying to hide her face – she had not the benefit of a veil or a parasol – as they bowled down the street with Sophy professing that she wanted 'to see the Bow Window I hear so much of'.

After surveying St James's once more, turn right on Jermyn Street, which is still famous for its exclusive men's tailors and other elegant shops and galleries. Turn right again on Bury Street. At the bottom you will be on King Street and almost opposite the site of the most select social venue in Regency London – Almack's Assembly Rooms. Unfortunately the building now at numbers 26–28 bears little resemblance to the original. Almack's was presided over by its dictatorial patronesses – the aristocratic Countess Leiven, Lady Jersey, Lady Sefton, Mrs Drummond Burrell, Emily Cooper and Princess Esterhazy – and one could go there only if one had been approved by these ladies and presented with vouchers. It was the goal of every social aspirant to enter these portals. The patronesses were extremely strict, however, and the young ladies had to prove they were of good 'ton' before they could succeed. Even Letty in *April Lady*, who thought it very 'slow' realized the importance of being granted vouchers to Almack's, and that any lady who failed was 'socially damned'. Many of the gentlemen found Almack's dull because it offered nothing stronger than ratafia and tea, and gaming was only allowed for very moderate stakes. Mr Temple-combe, in *Cousin Kate*, referred to the only evening he came here as 'the most insipid evening' he'd spent in his whole life. The pompous Lord Bridlington, on the contrary, approved of Almack's staid atmosphere.

Woe betide, too, anyone who arrived late, because the doors were resolutely shut at 11 p.m. The correct dress was also a requisite for entrance, and gentlemen were expected to appear in knee breeches and a chapeau-bras. Peregrine had to be sent home at the last minute to change when Mrs Scattergood discovered he was wearing pantaloons. She warned him to hurry as

A Regency dandy in evening wear

——————◆——————

the doors would close at eleven sharp and no one else would be allowed in – no matter who they were! When Freddy Standen visited Almack's to look for his sister Meg, not only was he 'beautiful to behold' in his correct evening dress but he was also one of those people who would never be asked to show his voucher. Not outrageous or outstanding in any way, he was very popular and welcomed everywhere for his good taste and charming, solicitous manners.

Having gained admission to this exclusive institution was not sufficient to enjoy all of its entertainments. Waltzing became acceptable at Almack's after it was introduced there by the society leader, the Countess Leiven, but until a young lady had proven herself and gained the approbation of one of the patronesses she was not allowed to participate in what many considered to be a rather 'fast' form of dancing. All the other dances of the times – the country dances, the quadrilles, the cotillion and the minuet – ensured a safe distance between the couples. But the waltz, as so many of the heroines were to discover, required a proximity to the male sex that was as heady as it was unusual for the closely chaperoned girls.

Despite the supposed strictness and superciliousness of the patrons of Almack's, they usually approved of the heroines in our novels. The 'Grand' Sophy was granted vouchers to Almack's by the Countess Leiven, despite her reckless gallop in the park. Miss Judith Taverner was 'passed' by Lady Jersey and Mrs Drummond Burrell, but upon arriving here she didn't think that all the fuss was worth it. The refreshments, consisting as they did of 'tea, orgeat and lemonade, with cakes and bread and butter' seemed rather minimal. The rooms weren't terribly grand, and whist was played for only sixpenny points. At the beginning of *Frederica*, the heroine breathlessly begged Lord Alverstoke to sponsor them into Almack's, and she was disappointed when he replied, 'You are aiming at the moon, Miss Merriville. No introduction of mine would help you to cross that hallowed threshold!' It was only by bribing his sister with a ball for her plain daughter Jane that Alverstoke was able to convince her to acquire the important vouchers for the Merrivilles.

Many of the young girls in the novels were fresh from the countryside and had only just come out. They often attended more informal parties to familiarize themselves with society and to make a few acquaintances before being 'pitch-forked' into the ton at Almack's. As the worldwise Lady Bridlington said in *Arabella*, there was nothing so unpleasant as coming to Almack's and not knowing a soul. The haughty Oliver Carleton in *Lady of Quality* complained that Almack's was 'choke-full of callow schoolroom misses' and he had no intention of letting his ward Lucilla make one of their number.

Many people in *Friday's Child* pitied Sherry's new wife Hero, who had been nicknamed 'The Nobody' by some malicious tongues – and both Lady Sefton and Lady Jersey decided to provide her with the essential vouchers so that she could have her chance to prove herself. Sherry himself was very conscious of his obligations, and said he'd better escort her there the first time she visited.

Almack's, as we have seen, was not a gentleman on the town's chosen way of spending the evening, as it was considered rather slow. Even Venetia, in the novel of the same name, said that when she was 'young' it was her greatest ambition to attend the Assemblies at Almack's but from everything she had heard she now believed they must be 'amazingly dull'.

Almack's features so many times in the novels that it is impossible to recount all the many diverting scenes that occurred here. Suffice it to mention briefly just a few of them. No avid reader will forget Judith Taverner's first visit to these assembly rooms. Incensed that she had been nicknamed 'The Milkmaid' because of her blonde beauty, she had a decided martial light in her eyes. Even more provoked by the fact that everyone told her she had to gain Mr Brummell's approval, she ended up confiding in the quiet, well-dressed stranger who sat down beside her at the Assembly. After roundly criticizing Mr Brummell and all such arbiters of fashion, she was appalled to discover later that she was talking to the great man himself!

Another *faux pas* at Almack's was partly the cause of all the conflict in the novel *Sylvester*. Phoebe Marlow was not only amazed that the Duke of Salford was coming to make her an offer but she was also horrified. After he had cut her at Almack's she made him the villain of the novel she'd written. Even Sherry, in *Friday's Child*, became reconciled to the insipidity of Almack's when he found such lively entertainment as Lord Wrotham being 'cut out' during a dance with the Incomparable Miss Milborne by Sir Mark Ravensby, and the subsequent behaviour of the handsome, hot-tempered lord. But it was right on King Street, outside Almack's, that Sir Ravensby got his come-uppance when he was approached by a poor lady with a baby bundled in her arms. Much embarrassed in front of his friends, Sir Ravensby, like the cad we know he was, disclaimed all knowledge of paternity. Hero, her pity excited, begged Sherry to let them take the woman and child home, an act which planted in Sir Ravensby a desire for revenge on Hero – which he exacted later in the novel.

Arabella had the privilege of being asked to dance her first waltz by Mr Beaumaris under circumstances which made all the other ladies green with envy. It was while they were dancing that Mr Beaumaris felt a 'stir of something in his heart' and perceptive readers know that this bastion of boredom and bachelorhood was at last beginning to be conquered!

Leaving Almack's and its memories behind, turn up Duke Street. On the corner of Duke Street and King Street was the Kings' Arms which was owned by Thomas Cribb, champion heavyweight of England. Here was the famous

Cribb's Parlour to which only the privileged were allowed entrance. The professional prizefighters, the amateurs and all who were devotees of the sport came – as Georgette Heyer says – from titled gentlemen to coalheavers. Farnaby in *Regency Buck* had to be content with the main tap room and it was here that Worth conducted his enigmatic interview with him.

Mr Rivenhall, one of the heroes who didn't aspire to the social graces, chose in *The Grand Sophy* to decline his sister Cecilia's invitation to Almack's and go instead to 'blow a cloud' with some friends at Cribb's Parlour. Nell Cardross was relieved to remember – when she saw Cardross hadn't changed for dinner – that he was not dining at home but off to Cribb's Parlour. Bertram, Arabella's brother, was lucky enough to handle the 'Champion's famous silver cup' which he'd won in his last fight against Molyneaux, 'The Black', several years ago.

Kitty Charing knew in *Cotillion* that her French cousin Camille, otherwise known as the Chevalier d'Evron, must have been respectable because he had lodgings in this street. It was here that Freddy Standen came to persuade the Chevalier that his only hope of achieving happiness was to elope with Olivia Broughty. Claud Darracott, in *The Unknown Ajax*, lived a frustrating life because he had a natural bent for interior decoration, a skill for which he found little scope at his two modest rooms in this street. He exercised his talent by advising ladies of fashion how to give a 'new touch' to their rooms, and hence eagerly awaited the opportunity to indulge in the decorating of a whole house for his cousin Hugo.

Back on Jermyn Street, walk along past the Princes Arcade on your left to Duke of York Street and turn right down it. This brings you into St James's Square. St James's Square was the nucleus from which the rest of the West End has grown. This square is still elegant and quiet, but few of the original houses line its sides. In the Regency period the square did not contain a garden in the centre but was paved and had a somewhat stagnant pool in the middle. Sir Richard Wyndham, creator of the Wyndham Fall, lived here. Three of his closest relatives took possession of his yellow saloon at the beginning of *The Corinthian* and threatened to remain there all day in order to persuade his lordship that it was time he married. It was back to this house that they came a day or two later – only to discover that Sir Richard had disappeared leaving only the provoking clues of a 'paisley shawl, a crumpled cravat, and some short strands of guinea-gold hair'.

After strolling around the square, exit by Charles II Street on the east side. This will bring you out again onto Regent Street.

CHAPTER II

BOND STREET AND BEAUX:
The East Side of Mayfair

Starting again at Piccadilly Circus, stroll down Piccadilly itself. Piccadilly, which runs down to Hyde Park Corner and flanks Green Park, was as busy in Georgette Heyer's Regency days as it is now. We shall be emerging into this street several times as we traverse the east and west sides of Mayfair, but now is as good a time as any to place this wide thoroughfare in its Regency setting. Piccadilly must have been a challenging street for young men. Dysart, Nell Cardross's rackety young brother in *April Lady*, was famous for walking the length of Piccadilly on a pair of stilts. For a bet, he also tried to drive a wheelbarrow down this street whilst blindfolded. And, of course, remember Jessamy on his pedestrian curricle creating chaos here in *Frederica*!

Coming up on your left is Hatchards, probably the most famous bookshop in the world. Established in 1797, and originally at number 173, it moved to its present location in 1801; hence, this is the actual site to which the Regency customers would have come. Hatchards was patronized by everyone of note – including the Duke of Wellington – and there used to be a bench outside the shop on which the footmen could rest while they awaited their masters and mistresses who shopped inside.

Many of the characters visited this famous bookstore, and we can browse through the books just as they did. Amongst these characters was the Viscount Desford in *Charity Girl* who decided that he needed a guide to Harrogate before

heading north. Unable to find one specific to Harrogate itself, he ended up with
A Guide to All the Watering and Seabathing Places, complete with 'tasteful Views,
numerous maps, town plans, and itineraries'. It was here in Hatchards that Kitty
Charing bought a book – *The Picture of London: A Guidebook to all the Monuments
and Other Places of Interest* – that was to be the scourge of Freddy Standen's life in
Cotillion.

One of the first places in London that Miss Taverner from *Regency Buck*
visited was Hatchards, 'with its bow windows filled with all the latest publications'. Miss Taverner obviously loved reading and she imagined her favourite
authors patronizing the shop. So delighted was she to find it was close to where
they were staying that Mrs Scattergood began to worry that Judith might be
bookish.

Cross the street, with care, and on your right you will see a cobbled driveway
leading into Albany. Virtually unchanged since its transformation from the
Duke of York's house to sets of chambers in 1802, it is the first example of
service flats in London. Not only was its intellectual, clublike atmosphere highly
desirable with many of the famous men of letters (for example Byron and Monk

Burlington Arcade, London

Lewis) but Georgette Heyer gave sets of rooms to a few of her characters. Albany has an additional interest for us because Georgette Heyer herself moved here in 1943 and made it her home until the arduous flights of stairs were no longer manageable.

Captain Ware in *The Foundling* rented a set of rooms in Albany. Georgette Heyer described the cosiness of them – with their classic shape, small iron balcony and burning fire, and how they were littered with manly paraphernalia. It was here that the Captain's father found the Duke of Sale's ring in Ware's drawer and became more worried than ever that his son had something to do with Sale's disappearance. Captain John Staple's friend Wilfrid Babbacombe in *The Toll-Gate* also had rooms here.

Go down Piccadilly past the Royal Academy on your right until you come to the Burlington Arcade; turn into it. The arcade was a favourite promenade for Regency bucks. Although not mentioned in the novels, in this classic remnant of Regency England one can certainly feel like a Georgette Heyer heroine out on a shopping spree. This is one of several such arcades in the area, and each is a pristine example of the period. Commissioned by Lord George Cavendish in 1812 the Burlington Arcade remained in his family's hands until 1926. This Arcade still has its beadle – in uniform – to ensure proper conduct in its precincts. As you enter, make sure you read the original rules. If you are lucky you will see the beadle telling off a young boy or girl who has had the audacity to run in the arcade or make too much noise. As you walk through the Arcade, notice not only the shops with their curved glass fronts but also the lighting and the attractive roof. The shop at number 50 is particularly interesting as it sells velvet slippers embroidered with crests and monograms – just like the slippers that Arabella worked so hard on as a 'thank-you' present for her uncle before she left for London.

Coming out of the Burlington Arcade, go up Cork Street, which is almost opposite. In *The Reluctant Widow*, the reprobate Eustace – who had suffered fatal wounds from a brawl and had been married on his deathbed to the reluctant Elinor Rochdale – kept rooms in this street. In *Regency Buck*, Mr Fitzjohn, Peregrine's first real friend in London, whom he had met at the prize fight outside Grantham, also had lodgings here. Captain Crake, Farnaby's second, came to his rooms to arrange the details of the duel with Peregrine. Mr Fitzjohn who had imbibed much worldly knowledge from his father soon realized that Captain Crake was 'not one whom any gentleman would desire to have for a second in an affair of honour'.

Cork Street leads to Clifford Street. Unfortunately this whole area is not as rich in Regency buildings as other parts of London. There are many new, very slick, glass-dominated structures, and even many of the older buildings date from just after the period in which we are interested. It is harder to immerse ourselves in the past here. Turn right on Clifford Street. Bertram in *Arabella* rushed off to Clifford Street to visit his friend Mr Scunthorpe's tailor so that he could get 'a new touch'. Bertram felt he couldn't spend his money to better advantage; also, there was the added benefit of being able to put it all 'on tick'.

If you turn left into Savile Row, this will bring you out on Conduit Street, where you should turn left again. Alverstoke, in *Frederica*, recommended Miss Starke in Conduit Street as the best milliner in London, so Frederica took her divinely beautiful sister Charis there to purchase some fashionable bonnets. The blonde Charis looked exquisite in everything she tried on, from the 'daring hat à la Hussar' to Miss Starke's *pièce de résistance* 'with its extravagant crown, its huge, upstanding poke, and its cascade of curled plumes'. The prices, however, were as extravagant as the hats, and Charis said she was quite happy to buy the less expensive 'Satin Straw' she'd seen in Bond Street. Being a woman of sound business sense, Miss Starke rapidly calculated how much new business she would get if those in the 'first circles' were to see Charis admirably displaying her most treasured concoctions. Not having been so crude as to actually *suggest* that Charis mention where she bought her hats, Miss Starke nonetheless allowed the Misses Merriville to leave her establishment gleeful over the purchase of three bonnets for the price of one.

Weston, one of the premier tailors of the Regency period also had premises in Conduit Street. It was he who made the well-cut coats which hugged the figures of Georgette Heyer's heroes so snugly they looked as if they were moulded to their bodies. Limmer's Hotel was situated here and this was where the 'Pets of the Ring' and the Corinthians who patronized them, were to be found. Dysart was a regular visitor and Bertram made a point of visiting this haunt whilst he was in London.

From Conduit Street go up St George Street to Hanover Square. This is where St George's, the church where Sherry and Hero were to be married by special licence at 2 o'clock, can be found. Until recently this was still *the* place for society weddings. Hero barely made it on time, as she had persuaded her escort, Mr Ringwood, to spend part of the morning at the Pantheon Bazaar. So productive was this shopping expedition that when they arrived at the church they could not dismiss the hackney as it contained so many packages. We can imagine Sherry and his cousin, the Honourable Ferdy Fakenham, waiting in the church porch and Georgette Heyer describes them with their 'blue coats, pale pantaloons, gleaming hessians, uncomfortably high shirt collars, and exquisitely arranged cravats'. Because Ferdy was the 'very Tulip of Fashion' he also had 'a long ebony cane, lavender gloves, and a most elegant buttonhole of clove pinks'. Again, as with many of the streets in this area, Hanover Square now contains many newish buildings, and only such ones as numbers 20 and 24 retain its former grace.

From Hanover Square, go left towards New Bond Street, which becomes Old Bond Street further down. Little of the architecture is original to our period, but it is not difficult to imagine this street as the hub of Mayfair in Regency London. This is the street that gave its name to a type of man – the Bond Street beau. In *Venetia*, Georgette Heyer described Bond Street as 'the most fashionable lounge in town'. It had everything: the most wonderful shops (as it still has today); the Pinks of the town made it 'the' street on which to strut; the Corinthians came to the famous boxing saloon; and everyone flocked to its famous libraries, particularly Hookham's. Not only would the pavements be crowded with the smart people, but the road would be full of every kind of coach, from barouches to whiskeys. It was highly unlikely that one could travel down this street either on foot or in a carriage without encountering *someone* one knew.

It was with this in mind that Venetia accepted the invitation to be escorted by her socially outcast stepfather, Sir Lambert. Sir Lambert was an impressive figure with the large build and protruding eyes of the royal princes. With his distinctive clothes and gallantry, he was significant enough a man to draw attention anywhere. He helped Venetia choose a muslin and, under the guise of buying a piece or two of jewellery for Lady Steeple, acquired a pretty brooch of aquamarines for Venetia. Coming out of the jeweller's, they were lucky enough to run into the strait-laced Edward Yardley. Venetia's association and conduct with Sir Lambert served to depress his pretensions to her hand forever and he left London in a huff. Venetia's plan was working well!

Nell Cardross, in *April Lady*, was being driven along Bond Street as she had 'a few trifling purchases to make', when, fortunately, she spotted her brother Dysart wearing pantaloons of an 'aggressive yellow'. Despite his fecklessness, Nell was always convinced he could help her, and she desperately needed to find the £300 to pay for her expensive court dress of 'Chantilly lace' before her husband found out about the unpaid bill. Dysart, with his usual want of tact, was too outspoken in front of the servants, and she had to give him a pinch to warn him to be discreet until they reached her home. And it was while sitting in her 'Mama's barouche' in front of a shop on this street that Miss Milbourne – the Incomparable – of *Friday's Child* saw Stacy parading down the street and she discovered how jealous he was of George Wrotham's attentions to Hero.

As Georgette Heyer said, Fate took a hand in Phoebe's affairs in *Sylvester* as she carried out some errands for Lady Ingham in Bond Street. She came across Ianthe and her child Edmund and was invited to return home with them in order to have a 'comfortable chat'. Ianthe took the opportunity to pour out all of her complaints about Sylvester, thus inadvertently drawing even closer resemblances between real life and the novel Phoebe had written.

When Alverstoke ran into Frederica, in the novel of the same name, in Bond Street, and found her unaccompanied, he was very angry about her lack of circumspection and was not at all reassured when she said she was to meet her aunt in Hookham's Library. He called her a 'green girl', and told her that if this was how she was going to behave she'd have to find another sponsor. Traditionally women only shopped in this street in the morning when the Beaux were not yet up. Even then they made sure they were accompanied by a footman or some other form of escort.

As we have already begun to see, the ladies came to Bond Street to shop and go to the libraries. One of the first things that the Viscount Sheringham did when he brought Hero to London was to take her to a 'mantua-maker's' in this street – 'an establishment where he was not unknown' – and hand over his espoused to be completely refitted. Hero was ecstatically happy with all of her new finery, and Sherry had to remonstrate with her for hugging him in public.

As you walk down the street, notice some of the older shops, such as Herbert Johnson at number 26 and Tessier, the silver and goldsmiths. Opposite this shop, on the front of number 147, is a blue plaque commemorating the fact that Nelson once lived here. He, of course, did not feature in the novels but he was often mentioned.

Many characters combined some shopping with a visit to Hookham's Library. As Judith Taverner said to her cousin Bernard upon meeting him here, 'I believe one is sure of meeting everyone at Hookham's, soon or late.' Georgette Heyer introduced a note of reality here by having Judith discover the novel *Sense and Sensibility* by Jane Austen, and read a very telling passage to her cousin. It was in Hookham's Library that Venetia thought she heard someone saying that the queen was not expected to survive the week, a titbit of gossip that she was able to divert her aunt's attention with at nuncheon.

At number 13, near the bottom of the street, was the famous Jackson's boxing saloon. Most of Georgette Heyer's mature heroes were on sparring terms with the great boxer, despite the fact that many of them presented such polished appearances that the heroines could be forgiven for not realizing they indulged in such manly exercise. It was also the desire of every young blade to be invited to try to 'pop' Jackson's 'cork', though Freddy in *Cotillion* did not share this ambition.

Jackson was famous throughout England for having beaten the great Mendoza, in record time in his last three fights. He was known as Gentleman Jackson because, unlike most fighters, he also had intelligence and pleasing manners. Many people came, for a fee, to spar and take instruction at his establishment, but only a lucky few were allowed the privilege of engaging with Jackson himself. Mr Scunthorpe, in his friendly fashion, introduced Bertram to the boxing school and while practising there with the single-stick, Bertram was overjoyed by the fact that Jackson deigned to notice him. The Marquis of Alverstoke in *Frederica* was kind enough to give Harry, Frederica's eldest brother, his personal card to present to Jackson. Harry, being very fond of boxing, thought this '*devilish* good' of him.

Judith Taverner, who despised her guardian Worth for being too much the dandy, was amazed to see him coming out of Jackson's. Peregrine was also surprised, especially when he realized that Worth had actually been sparring! Peregrine himself, came here to the saloon the day before his planned duel and forgot his own troubles whilst boxing. Charles Rivenhall too, in *The Grand Sophy*, came here to spar with Gentleman Jackson in order to work off his fury at finding Sophy driving his chestnut horse; in his case it was only marginally successful.

At bottom of Old Bond Street turn right onto Piccadilly and then take a sharp right onto Albemarle Street. The Clarendon Hotel was situated here. Like Brown's Hotel it had an entrance both on this street and on New Bond Street. It was renowned for having the best French dinner in town, for a price! Remember how Edward Yardley took Venetia and Mrs Hendred here for a special evening out, although Venetia was not at all keen to go. It was to this august establishment that Lady Broome, in *Cousin Kate*, brought Kate Malvern before whisking her away to mysterious Staplewood in the countryside. Over a very select dinner created by Jacquard in a private parlour overlooking Albemarle Street, 'Aunt Minerva' told Kate something of the history of the place she was going to and the pride she felt in its heritage.

Berkeley Square, London

In *Charity Girl* Viscount Desford drew up 'his sweating team', having driven like the wind to deliver Cherry Steane to the safekeeping of her grandfather – Lord Nettlecombe – whose town residence was here. Much to the horror of them both, the house was shuttered up and the knocker missing from the door: a sure sign that the occupants were away! Lord and Lady Buxted lived here in one of the houses until Lord Buxted died and his wife felt it encumbent upon her – for reasons of 'economy' – to leave her beautiful house. In the novel *Sylvester,*

Ianthe stayed on this street with her parents, Lord and Lady Elvaston, when she and her son Edmund left Chase without Sylvester's permission. Peregrine also ended up spending a great deal of time here as this was where the Fairfords lived 'in good style'.

As you walk up Albemarle Street, don't forget to explore the Royal Arcade on your right, again distinguished by its light, arched ceiling with the many skylights and the large lamp-holders hanging down its length. At the top of Albemarle Street, turn round and look back down the way you have come. St James's Palace is framed in a silk-screen haze at the end, just as it was over one hundred and fifty years ago.

Leaving Albemarle Street, turn left onto Grafton Street and left again. Then, taking the first right will bring you out onto Berkeley Street with Berkeley Square to your right. Pause and look across at the west side of the square which has retained many of the lovely old Georgian houses. Walking round the square, you will see that many of them still have the lamp-holders outside, and numbers 43, 44 and 50 still have the snuffers. The square, bound by railings, is large and green and open to the public. Lady Broome, in one of her bitter moods of reminiscence, recalled how Sir Timothy bought a house for her here when they were first married, but after three years she was forced to retire to the countryside with him when his health failed – forcing her to forsake fashionable life forever.

The Marquis of Alverstoke lived in this square and it was to his door that Frederica and her siblings came whenever they got themselves into a scrape. One of Alverstoke's neighbours was the Earl of Jersey, whose wife was one of the famous patronesses of Almack's. Known behind her back as 'Silence', she found it an insoluble problem, when invited to dress parties at Alverstoke House, to decide whether to 'call out one's carriage, or to demean oneself by walking some fifty yards to the party'. The Omberslys in *The Grand Sophy* lived here in the square and it is easy to imagine the dramatic arrival of Sophy with her entourage. This exciting event was witnessed by almost the entire family – the children peered through the railings of the garden in the middle of the square where they had been playing at bat and ball, and the elder members who had just come back after driving in the Park were in the hallway of the house. Sophy did not travel light on this occasion. Her chaise 'with a mountain of baggage on the roof' was drawn by four horses and accompanied by two outriders, men whose task it was to protect the traveller from highwaymen. Her groom rode behind leading Sophy's splendid black horse Salamanca. The joy of the children was complete when they saw Sophy descend from her carriage with a sleek Italian greyhound and a little monkey wearing a scarlet jacket. The adults were rather overcome: instead of the quiet little thing they had expected, they were confronted with a Junoesque figure swathed in furs and obviously very certain of herself.

In *Cotillion* Freddy arranged for his newly 'betrothed' Kitty to stay with his sister Meg here in Berkeley Square, to the satisfaction of all concerned. Meg's husband was on a mission to China and Meg needed a chaperon so that she wouldn't have to go to stay with one of her strict relatives. Kitty was grateful for the hospitality because the Standen house was full of measles and she certainly didn't want to go back to the countryside before she'd had time to carry out her plan in London.

Gunters was also situated in this square – an establishment known not only for the quality of the food it provided, but also renowned for its famous ices. The blocks of ice that Gunters used were buried in the ground under the cellars of the square. When Mr Chawleigh, in *A Civil Contract*, hired a whole building in the Strand for everyone to watch the processions of the Allied Sovereigns to the Guildhall, he ensured the comfort of the party by 'ordering a large and varied luncheon from Gunters'. Elsewhere in the novels people were always comparing the ices they'd had elsewhere to the ones that were available here.

Lady Ombersley in *The Grand Sophy* was spared the necessity of worrying about food for her large parties while cousin Mathilda was alive for she had always taken care of these matters with Gunters. And on her mad shopping spree before leaving for Ravenshurst, Lady Denville in *False Colours* – ordered amongst other comestibles 'a large quantity of wafers' from the famous store, though Mr Dawlish, her cook, was rather snobbish about them and said that he preferred to make his own. After Mr Hethersett in *April Lady* rescued Nell Cardross from the doorstep of Mr King, the moneylender, he suggested that Nell might like to go to Gunters and have an ice, but Nell was not interested in the solace of the proposed diversion.

Before leaving Berkeley Square look down Bruton Street which leads off the square on the northeast side. The fashionable modiste Madame Franchot, whom Alverstoke had recommended to Frederica and her sister Charis, was located in this short street. Another modiste – Madame Lavalle – had her premises in Bruton Street. It was her desire to retire and collect as much of the money owing to her as possible that catapulted Nell Cardross into all of her troubles in *April Lady*. Madame Fanchon in *Cotillion* worked here too, and Kitty Charing came to her elegant establishment. Being ushered into a showroom carpeted with an Aubusson and furnished with gilt spindly chairs, Kitty realized that Madame was going to be very expensive. With the contrivance of Meg however, Kitty discovered that she could afford a few of the dresses she fell in love with.

Leave Berkeley Square at the northern end and head up Davies Street; not a particularly distinguished street, but as you walk you will get a better picture of older London if you glance down the side mews. The Three Kings Yard is on the left and Brooks Mews on your right. Charles Trevor only managed to get as far as Davies Street when he tried to return the 'Baluchistan' hound Lufra to the Merrivilles. Lufra however had decided that Charles was the enemy, and squatted down on his haunches and refused to budge.

At the top of Davies Street is Bond Street tube station where we shall end this walk.

CHAPTER III

'AT HOME':
The West Side of Mayfair

*I*n Regency London, Mayfair was the centre of life for the 'ton'. As we can see in Georgette Heyer's novels, most of its well-to-do members had townhouses here, and the streets were lined with their imposing mansions or elegant smaller abodes. The streets would have been alive with the sound of horses and carriages of all descriptions, with many servants in evidence cleaning steps, and polishing the decorative knockers on the doors – an indication that their masters and mistresses were in residence. As you wander in Mayfair today, the streets will be far more deserted than they were then, as so many of the buildings have been converted for commercial usage.

Start at the top of Duke Street which is just west, beyond Bond Street tube station. Rebuilding, extensive renovation, and bombing have all taken their toll in this area, and it is difficult to catch glimpses of the once elegant past. Go down Duke Street until you reach Grosvenor Square. The first major turning on your left, running off from Grosvenor Square, is Brook Street. Now largely commercial, Brook Street, especially the end near Grosvenor Square, was an extremely desirable place to live at the beginning of the nineteenth century.

Lord Worth, in his high-handed manner, had procured the lease for a house here as a suitable place for his wards, the Taverners, to live in while they were in town. Judith Taverner, who was used to ordering her own life, bitterly resented

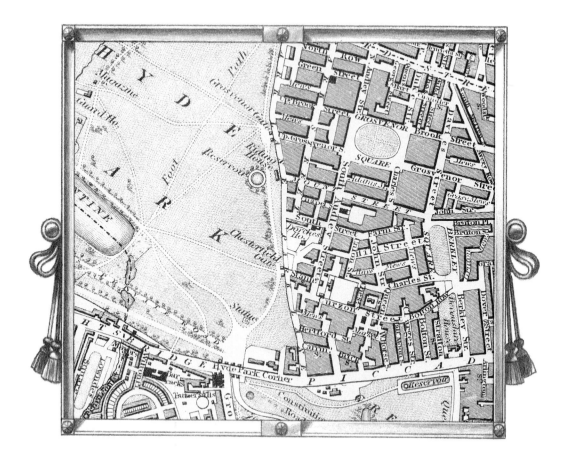

this autocratic dealing but, biting her lip, had to admit that she didn't yet know London well enough to decide where she would like to be located. Mrs Scattergood, who was completely 'up to snuff', pronounced that it was 'a charming situation'. Miss Taverner was irritated to find no fault with the house, it being 'admirable in every respect' with spacious rooms that were attractively furnished. It was not long before the cream of society was paying her morning visits – among them their leader, Mr Brummell, whom she had so unwittingly insulted at Almack's. Even the Duke of Clarence honoured her with his presence. Unfortunately, he arrived while she had her uncle the Admiral with her, but to Judith's relief she found his rather rough manners underwent a 'distinct change' in the presence of royalty. The Duke's visits became a regular event until he made Miss Taverner an offer which she refused with as much circumspection as she could.

It was here, from their house in Brook Street, that Miss Taverner and her

Judith Taverner's curricle

♦

brother set out in separate curricles on their ill-fated race to Brighton. Judith's decision to persist in this foolish endeavour threw Mrs Scattergood into such a state that she sat down 'plump upon her best bonnet'!

One of Brook Street's less appealing habituées was Miss Wraxton, Mr Rivenhall's strait-laced fiancée in *The Grand Sophy*. Miss Wraxton's family house, as befitting the character of its inhabitants, was described by Georgette Heyer as 'somewhat cheerless'. Another of the heroes was almost forced into an engagement with someone else who lived in Brook Street. In *The Corinthian*, urged on by his family to do his duty and offer for Melissa Brandon, Sir Richard Wyndham drove over to Lord Saar's family house in this street. The Saars were all notorious gamblers and had for a long time past counted on the generosity of Sir Richard's prospective wedding settlements to release them from their difficulties. Fortunately, the coldly pragmatic nature of Melissa's response to Sir

Richard's visit enabled him to leave without committing himself by making an offer. Melissa believed that financial calculations and family name were the only legitimate concerns in a proposed marriage, whereas Sir Richard was unfashionable enough to hope that his wife might also love him. Later, as Sir Richard wandered in his very inebriated state through the dawn-lit Brook Street on his way home from his club, he kissed his fingers in the direction of the Saar house and ironically referred to Melissa as 'my gentle bride!'

Dysart, Nell Cardross' brother in *April Lady*, was trapped into dining in Brook Street by 'Old Mother Wenlock', who wanted him to meet her niece, who was supposedly a 'ravishing girl' but who turned out to be a mere dowd. Lord Bodlington in *The Reluctant Widow* lived in Brook Street. He tried to persuade the new 'Mrs Cheviot' to shut up the mysterious house, 'Highnoons', in the country – which she had inherited on the death of her 'husband' – in order to move in with him here. Olivia Broughty's grand relations in *Cotillion* also lived here. They, to her disappointment, had not accorded her a cordial welcome, and hence she and her mother had to resort to living in Kensington beyond the pale as far as the 'ton' were concerned. In *Venetia* Damerel had a house here, and even Venetia's outcast mother and stepfather once resided on this street before the ostracism they encountered forced them to move to the Continent.

As well as being on the corner of Duke and Brook Streets, you are obviously now facing Grosvenor Square. This was one of the largest and most fashionable of the squares in which to have an address in Regency London. The square was salubrious from the start – the garden being laid out in the centre by Sir Richard Grosvenor in 1725. As the houses were built, the elite – all had titles or were MPs – were quick to move in. It is an imposing place, and today still ranks as one of the most prestigious addresses in Mayfair. It is a rare resident who lives here now, however, as most of the square is taken up with the streamlined modern embassy blocks, that have completely replaced the original Georgian houses.

In Georgette Heyer's novel *April Lady*, the Earl of Cardross' splendid town house was located on the square. Here his young wife, Nell, lived with his lordship and his unruly half-sister Letty. Nell had her own apartments which Cardross had decorated especially for her. Her bedroom's centrepiece was a 'tent-bed with rose-silk curtains upheld by Cupids and garlands', and her boudoir was hung in blue and silver brocade. It was to their house here that the very correct Mr Allandale reluctantly called, hoping to gain Cardross' permission to marry Letty before he had to leave for Brazil.

It was also from this house that the famous Cardross necklace – consisting of an 'awe-inspiring collection of emeralds and diamonds heavily set in gold' – disappeared. Nell was convinced that her brother Dysart had taken it in order to raise money for her; the Earl believed that Nell had pawned it, but it is the young Letty who was the real culprit. A bold young woman, who had been improperly brought up, she saw it as a perfectly acceptable way to raise the money she needed to enable her to elope with Allandale to the border.

In *Friday's Child*, Lord Sheringham, known to his friends as Sherry, had a family mansion in Grosvenor Square. Ringwood considered it a very 'good address', and advised Sheringham to set up his establishment here with his new wife Hero. He added, however, that the whole place would need to be redecorated and all the old furniture thrown out before it could be suitably habitable. Sherry's Uncle Prosper called it a 'draughty great mansion', but doubted whether any woman would throw up the chance of living in the best part of town.

Hero was terrified by the gloominess of the house with its old retainers – the furniture swathed in Holland covers and all the sombre oil paintings – 'huge armoirs, massive chandeliers, and draped curtains'. She was only too thankful when Sherry, thinking more about the logistics of living here, including the enormous expense of all the servants they would require, decided that Hero wouldn't be happy in such a house. Lord Sheringham, who himself was still rather young and not eager to lead the staid married existence befitting his rank, shocked his man of business by referring to Sheringham House as a 'curst gloomy hole . . . worse than Brooks'!'

Damerel explained to Venetia in the novel of the same name that the reason he was visiting his estates in Yorkshire was to escape from his aunts. The eldest he described as the 'most intimidating female you ever beheld'. She lived in a 'mausoleum' here in the Square, rarely leaving it but holding 'receptions very like the Queen's Drawing-Rooms'. A very eccentric lady who dressed badly and was neither amiable nor amusing, she had somehow convinced the ton that she was a 'second Lady Cork', and people thought it an honour to be invited to her 'salons'.

As you walk right round the square, or sit in the garden in the centre, recall Sir Bonamy who, as Lady Denville knew, led a very luxurious life, owning a mansion in Grosvenor Square as well as places in Brighton, Newmarket, York and Bath. The delightful nabob, Sir Thomas Bolderwood, in *The Quiet Gentleman* had a townhouse in this square which was reserved for all 'state' and 'flummery': their entertaining in the country being of a very impromptu and informal style.

Until her father, the Earl of Spenborough, died, Serena too, in *Bath Tangle*, was a frequent resident of their townhouse in the Square. Her last visit here was not a happy one, as she had come to prepare it for the new owners. Not only sad at having to relinquish her home, she was also hurt that the new Lady Spenborough had not had the grace to wait before inspecting it 'from cellars to attics'. The Earl of Spenborough's very young second wife Fanny had never felt very comfortable in the large houses at Milverley or Grosvenor Square, and she had been terrified at the dinners here when she had had to try and follow the quick-witted political discussions that were a regular part of the evening's entertainment – and a great stimulus to her sister-in-law Serena.

Having been all the way round the square, go up North Audley Street, which was where the Misses Berry lived in *April Lady*. Nell was left to pay them a morning visit by herself, as Letty claimed to have had a troubled night, and a toothache. As the Misses Berry were two rather difficult old ladies, Nell was a little suspicious about the toothache, especially when Letty was reluctant to see a dentist.

Turn left onto Green Street. Gerard Monksleigh and Emily Laleham rather spuriously discussed 'the rival merits of Green Street and Grosvenor Square as possible localities for the house of a rising politician', on the first stage of their elopement, thus diverting Emily's mind from her fear of being pursued. Hampden House, which is on the left side of the street, is one of the oldest buildings along here, having been built in 1730 and originally consisting of two houses, numbers 60 and 61. The Hampden family lived here from 1760 until 1833, and it is an excellent example of the type of house our characters would have owned. One of the interesting facts about houses built during that time is that because cement hadn't been invented, they used a mixture of bull's blood and straw which formed a very strong substance for the foundations of the buildings.

Mrs Dawtry, the mother of the beautiful but not very quick-witted Endymion, lived in this street. When Mr Trevor ruined his and Charis' plans for marrying secretly in a church in St Clement Danes, Endymion decided he had better dash back here immediately, as he expected 'she might be prostrated' by a letter he had left for her announcing his wedding. Alverstoke couldn't understand why he had written to her *before* the wedding, so Charles Trevor, almost unable to contain himself, carefully explained that Endymion was apparently worried that if he didn't write at once he would forget to do so afterwards!

The 'Incomparable' Miss Milborne lived here with her family in *Friday's*

Park Street, London

◆

Child. The Duchess of Severn very graciously deigned to make a formal morning call to the Milbornes, an event that caused the bettors to shorten the odds on the Beauty's most illustrious suitor, Severn, winning the field. It was also here in the Milborne house that Severn's rival, the tempestuous, handsome Lord Wrotham, who was everything that Severn was not, came visiting. Dismayed by her seeming predilection for Severn, Wrotham 'so far forgot himself as to seize her in his arms, enfolding her in a crushing embrace and covering her face with kisses'. Interrupted by the butler announcing more morning visits, this passionate behaviour did not advance him in the Incomparable's graces.

The dowager Lady Ingham, from the novel *Sylvester*, was described as living here in Green Street in a 'house bursting with all the furniture and ornaments' that she had removed from the family house when her son married. A somewhat eccentric lady of strong mind and supposed ills, she was someone who expected to get her own way in everything. Not knowing that the match was originally Lady Ingham's idea, Phoebe took refuge in her house, having run away from home at the thought of having to marry the grand, imperious Sylvester. We can imagine the chaise, all bespattered with mud, pulling up here late in the evening and Horwich, Lady Ingham's stiff old butler, looking askance at this unexpected guest who had the temerity to arrive at such an advanced hour.

Having strolled along Green Street, turn left onto Park Street. Off here is Lee's Place, and it is worth turning left into this quiet precinct. Although it is not mentioned in the novels, tucked away on the right-hand side behind what is the back of Hampden House is the Mayfair Cottage, which was built in 1723. Replete with a flower garden in front, this house is a forceful reminder of a time when the area was not so heavily urban. The cottage has obviously been restored, but do notice the old light sconces on the door. Back on Park Street, don't forget to glance down Woods Mews to the right. The number of mews in the area is eloquent testimony to the quantity of horses that were kept here by the ton, who set up their stables in town as a matter of course. Each gentleman or family, as we can see so often in the novels, kept several different types of carriages as well as riding horses.

On Park Street, at numbers 76 and 78, you can see two of the best examples of unspoilt Regency houses. Notice how narrow the doors are, the style of the letterboxes, and the small fanlights. The buildings are leaning slightly with age, and I hope by the time you read this they haven't been smartened up too much and had their character destroyed.

As you walk down Park Street, remember how enthralled and bewildered Arabella was when she first arrived in London with Miss Blackburn after the long journey from the north. Like many of the other heroines on their first visit to the metropolis, she was overwhelmed by all the noise and the people after the quiet of the country. The old family carriage, dirty after the long journey, stopped outside a house on this street that appeared 'overpoweringly tall' after the 'rambling two-storey countryhouses' she was used to. The drawing-room

was, of course, on the first floor, and Arabella was relieved to be led up to it on the grand flight of stairs by the stately butler, who was 'supported by only one footman'! Arabella was soon made to feel completely at home by the warm welcome she was given by Lady Bridlington, who was plump, good-natured and 'clasped' Arabella 'to her ample bosom'.

It was here in Park Street that the climbing boy was forced down the chimney and ended up in Arabella's bedroom. Not one to shirk her duty as a vicar's daughter, she immediately took it upon herself to improve his lot in life – a responsibility that finally fell upon Mr Beaumaris. Lady Serena stayed with her Aunt Theresa here on Park Street and had to endure an 'encroaching' visit from the new owner of her own family home.

Continuing down Park Street, don't forget to explore briefly Culross Street, to the left and right, which has some good period houses, especially numbers 12 and 14. The old Grosvenor Gate into the Park used to be at the Park Lane end of Culross Street. Upper Grosvenor Street crosses Park Street a little further on. A little way along to the right you can see a blue plaque commemorating the place where the two Sir Robert Peels – the son and Prime Minister – resided, both men who lived during the Regency period.

Back on Park Street, go down a little further and turn left onto Mount Street. Mount Street figured frequently in Georgette Heyer's novels, and it is unfortunate that many of the buildings now belong more to the latter half of the nineteenth century rather than to the beginning.

That elegant gentleman and leader of society, Mr Beaumaris, lived on Mount Street. Lord Fleetwood, his best friend, was horrified when he discovered that Robert was going to bring the wretched little climbing boy home, exclaiming 'everyone will think it's a by-blow of yours'. The Oversleys of *A Civic Contract* lived in this street too, and Adam spent much of his time before his 'arranged' marriage visiting the beautiful and highly strung Julia here. His last visit was not a happy one, as he had to break it to her that having inherited so many debts and encumbered estates he was no longer in a position to offer her his hand in marriage.

Despite the short distance between Hill and Mount Streets, Kit Fancot was driven in state to Mount Street in the family carriage on the evening he had seriously to begin his impersonation of his twin Evelyn. The Staveleys had all gathered here in their house, led by the autocratic Lady Staveley, to meet Cressida's betrothed. Evelyn's disappearance had caused his mother a great deal of worry until Kit's timely return from the Continent. For Kit's resemblance to his brother, and his natural diplomatic aplomb, enabled him to carry out the impersonation with only a few problematic moments; fortified by 'the excellent food and drink offered him', he was even emboldened to banter with Cressida.

Lord Lionel came to Mount Street in *The Foundling* to visit his old friend Sir Timothy Wainfleet. He hoped that Sir Timothy would be able to tell him truthfully what 'on-dits' were going round the town about his son's role in the disappearance of his cousin, the Duke of Sale. He found his friend 'huddled over a fire in his bookroom . . . wizened and alarmingly alert'. Much as it pained him to do it, Sir Timothy revealed that rumour held that Sale had been murdered and that Captain Ware was the chief suspect.

Freddy's parents in *Cotillion* lived in Mount Street, and it was here that he brought Kitty Charing to stay for her month's planned sojourn in London. Unfortunately, unbeknownst to him, the house was full of measles, and even the normally hospitable Lady Legerwood didn't feel she could cope with a visitor. His parents were also naturally surprised at his sudden engagement! Everyone will remember the inscrutable but interested look in his father's eyes as Freddy started to show a very competent side to his character. Having safely ensconced Kitty at his sister's house, Freddy had little further leisure to visit the parental home in the days ahead. He ended up having to spend all his time looking after Kitty by taking her about London.

Carlyon's sensible brother John lived in Mount Street in *The Reluctant Widow*, but Nicky, having been sent down from university, had no desire to come here and be lectured to. Lord Charlbury, who was convinced by Sophy that the only way to win Cecilia was to flirt with Sophy herself, was another Mount Street resident, as were the Wetherbys in *Sprig Muslin*. Lady Aurelia chose to remain at Darracott Place in *The Unknown Ajax* to keep an eye on her son Vincent, rather than return here to her home in Mount Street.

Having explored Mount Street, turn off it and walk down South Audley Street. On the left, behind the church, is a sanctuary of green – a restful spot in which to sit down for a while. The Mount Street Gardens used to be a cemetery, and you can still see the marks on the ground where the graves used to be.

Go down South Audley Street: this is a good place to look down through the railings of the houses into the old servants' areas. Just past the Grosvenor Chapel (which Nell Cardross attended on the Sunday she was too late to go to the Chapel Royal), in a short cul-de-sac, is an interesting house at number 23. As you turn left onto Farm Street, you will see the Punch Bowl, one of the few remaining public houses. There were, in Georgian times, very many public houses in this small area and they were patronized by the grooms, ostlers and other workers who were employed to keep all the horses and carriages of the gentry in good trim. The Old Farm House, which gave the street its name, is on the right-hand side, halfway down.

Turn right down Hay's Mews to Hill Street. Lady Denville's sons, the Fancots, had their townhouse here. We can imagine Kit arriving back from the Continent late at night, the street quite deserted. Despite pulling hard on the iron bell-pull, nobody answered his summons, and Kit was forced to contemplate other means of egress. Leaving his portmanteau by the front door and stripping off his greatcoat, Kit climbed up the outside of the house to the dining room window where he was able to throw up the sash and clamber inside. Another evening Kit was amused to see his mother escorted home by no less than four gallants, all eagerly clustered around her elegant sedan chair lined 'with pale green velvet' and vying for her attention.

Having paused to take in Hill Street, carry on down Hay's Mews past the Coach and Horses and on down to the public house bearing the unusual name 'I Am the Only Running Footman', on the corner of Charles Street. The historical associations of the name alone justify stopping here, but it was also mentioned in the novel *False Colours*. The twin brothers, Kit and Evelyn, had been desperately trying to concoct a story that would explain the exigencies of their situation – the wrong brother marrying Cressy! Having finally come up with a tale they thought would be convincing, Kit was horrified at the idea that they should be the ones to spread it. He assured his brother and his betrothed that all they had to do was acquaint their grooms Timber and Challow with 'the bare bones' of the story and give them a half an hour in the Running Footman after which time it would be all over London within a day – in various 'garbled versions'.

Just inside the door is a framed plaque explaining the role that the running footman played in the days of carriages; and on the wall to the left is a large painting – set slightly before the Regency period – depicting a running footman in action.

Charles Street still has the feel of the Regency, and houses like number 41 are typical of what one would have expected to see in the period. It is worth turning right out of the pub and walking to the end of Charles Street where it narrows considerably. To your right runs the attractive street called Chesterfield Hill. On one of the houses here you will see a blue plaque noting the place where the Duke of Clarence – of *Regency Buck* fame – lived at one time.

Backtrack slightly and turn into Chesterfield Street. Halfway down is a narrow white house in which Beau Brummell lived. Small and elegant, one can imagine it being the perfect abode for a single gentleman who led the ton in all matters of style. Beau Brummell had acquired his reputation by setting a fashion that was at once extremely simple but also very expensive. His absorption in sartorial perfection was such that he would spend at least five hours every morning at his toilet; but once having emerged, he would not give another thought to his dress.

Curzon Street, at the bottom of Chesterfield Street, confronts us with the business of the modern world; architecturally it is a mélange of the old and the new. Hero and Sherry condemned a house in Curzon Street as uninhabitable as it had 'a very ugly fireplace in the drawing-room'. The socially suspect Mrs Gillingham resided in Curzon Street, and when Hero questioned the propriety of attending her 'little card party', Mrs Huby reassured her by pointing out the elegance and style of Mrs Gillingham's gown and 'The address too . . . it is unexceptionable!' However, Hero's scruples were well-placed, and when she arrived at the 'slip of a house' on this street and was ushered in, her worst fears were confirmed. The company was strange to her, and she ended up losing far more than she could afford at the gaming tables.

The Duke of Sale in *The Foundling* had his town residence in Curzon Street: Sale House, the adjunct to his country property Sale Park. Tired of his title and the pomp and formality that accompanied it, the diffident Duke daydreamed

A Regency boot scraper

———————◆———————

about what life might be like if he had been born plain Mr Dash. So deep was he into this picture of a simpler existence that it came as a rude shock when his chaise swept into the forecourt of his house and he was confronted by its imposing portico and panoply of servants – all eager to ensure that the Duke had absolutely nothing to do for himself.

Before traversing the streets that run between Curzon Street and Piccadilly, it is worth taking some time to explore Shepherd Market, the fascinating area just below Curzon Street. This is the site of the original May Fair, which from the late seventeenth century was held on 1 May and lasted for fourteen or fifteen days. The demise of the Fair not only came about because of its reputation for bawdiness and violence, but also because of the sheer development going on around the area. Shepherd Market is still a maze of intimate streets that have a cosy, more lively appeal after the cool elegance of the rest of Mayfair.

Head down Half Moon Street and you can weave your way up and down through Clarges, Bolton and Stratton Streets. All these streets are somewhat narrow, and although enough of the older buildings still survive to make it worthwhile to move quickly through them, the new office buildings tend to ruin the eye's line and overshadow the streets.

Half Moon Street is of course embedded in the mind of any avid Georgette Heyer reader as the street where Sherry and Hero found the house in which they wanted to live and set up home here in a somewhat youthful and irresponsible fashion in *Friday's Child*. We can imagine the two returning from the hunting box in Leicestershire and arriving in Half Moon Street, 'at dusk one evening'. Hero was absolutely thrilled: 'Nothing could have been more charming or more tasteful than the disposition of the furniture in the little house.' The home was made complete by Mr Ringwood's present of a 'canary in a gilded cage'. Sherry, on the other hand, was brought to a halt by the staggering pile of bills reposing on his new kneehole desk. Neither of them had any idea of how to manage money, and Sherry was amazed at the amount Hero had spent on the furniture, 'but he handsomely made up his mind to level no reproach at her'.

At the end of Half Moon Street, bear left and turn into Clarges Street. Nell, heavily veiled, in *April Lady*, entered it at this point and halted after she had been walking about in Green Park, trying to summon up the necessary courage to face the moneylender Mr King. Modernized as it is today, it is difficult to pick out which 'discreet-looking house' could be the one where Mr King conducted his business. As you can tell, Clarges Street is not very long, and we can imagine Nell irresolutely pacing up and down until she was spotted by the loyal Mr Hethersett who was fortuitously visiting a friend on the opposite side of the street to Mr King. Just as Nell was about to mount the steps, she was halted by Mr Hethersett's salutation, and at his persuasion was forced to walk away, thus being 'rescued from the perils of Clarges Street'.

Bertram's dear friend Mr Scunthorpe, in *Arabella*, had lodgings in Clarges Street. Despite Felix Scunthorpe's lack of mental acuity, he was 'up to every rig and row in town!' and proceeded to impart as much of his town lore to Bertram as quickly as possible. It was not only his new tailoring that gave Bertram 'a new touch'. After an extremely full day and evening in the metropolis, Felix and Bertram were delivered here in a hackney to Felix's home where Bertram spent the little left of the night on his friend's sofa after 'a very bosky evening'.

Even though Lady Wyndham in *The Corinthian* owned a 'charming house' in Clarges Street, she always felt a slight sense of pique when visiting her son's much larger mansion in St James's Square. Clarges Street is also where Kate Malvern and her Papa in *Cousin Kate* had 'an elegant set of rooms' when things were going well financially for him.

The next street over is Bolton Street and at the far end, on the corner of Piccadilly, is where Watier's was situated in an 'unpretentious house which had once been a gaming establishment of quite a different order'. Watier's was probably the most prestigious club in town, and to belong to it 'the object of every aspirant to fashion'. Georgette Heyer explained in *April Lady* that it came into being when the Prince Regent suggested to Watier, one of his cooks, that he start an exclusive club offering the pick of the ton a place where they could get a good dinner, as the food at all the other London clubs was so dreadful. The idea took and Watier's, as it came to be called, 'blossomed' not only into a place where it was possible to enjoy congenial company and excellent food and wine, but also 'the most exclusive as well as the most ruinous of all London's gaming clubs'. Presided over by Mr Brummell, and with a bank of ten thousand, Hazard and Macao were the favoured games; play began at nine o'clock and continued all night. Dysart, who had an engagement to dine at Watier's and afterwards hazard his luck at the tables, did not intend 'to keep the best dinner in town waiting' by first going to see his sister Nell, despite her urgent plea for him to visit her.

Worth was, of course, a member of Watier's, and Peregrine finally caught up with him there after looking for him all over town. Unfortunately Peregrine ended up playing at his table and losing rather a lot of money to him, which was rather embarrassing for Worth as Peregrine was his ward.

The next street on the left is Stratton Street. Don't venture far down it, but remember the two young gentlemen, Mr Ringwood and the Honourable Ferdinand Fakenham, who sat in the front parlour of a house here, breakfasting after a somewhat inebriated night on the town. Georgette Heyer described Mr Ringwood's lodging as a true 'bachelor abode', full of 'snuff jars, cigars, and sporting paraphernalia'. The somnolence of their morning repast was broken

GEORGETTE HEYER'S REGENCY ENGLAND

only by the impetuous entrance of their friend Sherry, who wanted to know how to obtain a special licence. This startling piece of news penetrated even their 'castaway' brains.

Ironically, it was on another occasion later in the novel that Mr Ringwood and Ferdy were once again comfortably ensconced here in the lodgings when another unexpected visitor arrived. This time it was evening, and what with having a cold and the weather presaging sleet, Mr Ringwood felt a quiet dinner and a round of picquet at home with Ferdy would be more sensible than venturing out. Having been joined by Lord Wrotham, the three were well into the port and cards when a knock at the door heralded the arrival of Hero, with a pale, tear-stained face, birdcage in one hand and 'and ormolu clock clutched under the other arm'. Georgette Heyer painted an extremely amusing picture of the group as the gentlemen's inate sense of chivalry vied with their initial sense of outrage at this flagrant breach of ton. Every reader knows that ladies do not visit gentlemen's lodgings unescorted, if at all!

Having sampled the delights of Stratton Street, you really have now covered all the little nooks and crannies of Mayfair and can move on to the parks.

CHAPTER IV

THE LONDON PARKS:
Sylvan Settings

The London Parks, particularly St James's, Green Park, Hyde Park and Kensington Gardens, were then oases of green in the town, as they are now. They also provided the ton of Regency London with another important social venue and a place for exercise, ranging from a mild walk to driving or riding. Here too society imposed its rules. As Georgette Heyer said in *April Lady*, it was 'de rigueur for anyone of high fashion' to be seen walking, driving or riding in Hyde Park on a fine afternoon between the hours of five and six. At this time one could admire the 'exquisites on the Grand Strut', the ladies vying for the attention of these members of the dandy-set, and Rotten Row thronged with carriages and riders. The *hoi poloi* and the middle classes tacitly left these regions of the park to those of rank and fashion.

At a time when horses provided the main form of transportation, it is no wonder that people were judged on what they drove and rode. The style of vehicle they owned depended very much on the image they wanted to create, and their skill with the reins. Young Lady Cardross in *April Lady*, whose husband thought she had only married him for his money, was thrilled to receive a very smart barouche – in the very latest mode, with the wheels picked out in yellow – from her husband as a wedding present. The quality of the horses that pulled the vehicles were even more important, and Nell was lucky enough to have a pair of 'perfectly matched greys'. Having been used to riding in an old landaulet, she

A Phaeton

❖

knew she would be 'all the crack'! We can imagine her being driven round the Park with her sister-in-law Letty, not realizing that it was not the horses that were drawing all the attention, but the enchanting picture they made together – as the outspoken Letty pointed out – the one fair, the other dark. It was during one such drive that Mr Hethersett, the sartorial arbiter in this book, told Letty, much to her indignation, that the pink bows on her dress and the pink feathers in her hat were 'commonplace'. Cherry would be much better, he opined.

In *Arabella*, Lady Bridlington took her 'pretty protégée' driving in the Park in her barouche, and was somewhat surprised by the number of people who stopped the carriage to speak to them. She finally explained it to herself by believing that she had done such a wonderful job of letting it be known that she had Arabella staying with her. The omniscient reader, however, remembers the wonderful scene the heroine had had at Mr Beaumaris' hunting box where she informed him very mendaciously that she was 'cursed with a large fortune'. Unknown to Lady Bridlington, all the attention Arabella was receiving was not due to Arabella's enchanting smile nor to her own efforts as a hostess.

Sensible Jenny in *A Civil Contract* had a fine solution to stop the tongues wagging about Julia fainting when she saw Adam at a ball. Jenny proposed to drive Julia in the Park in her barouche. Not only would it show people that they were still good friends but, as unpretentious Jenny also admitted, if she drove alone she would only get two or three bows, as she knew so few people in London, but if the exquisite Julia joined her they would be 'mobbed'. Unlike the picture presented by Nell and Letty, Jenny and Julia were a study in contrasts of a different sort. Jenny was plump and unbecomingly dressed in 'Brunswick grey lustring'; Julia was frail and beautiful in 'a new walking-dress of French cambric'. As Jenny had foreseen – so many people acknowledged them and wished to exchange civilities that their progress was inordinately slow. While Jenny was secretly bored by the niceties of such social intercourse and thought it a waste of time, Julia happily came out of her depression and thrived on all the attention.

It was also the custom for gentlemen to invite ladies to go driving with them in their curricles. Alverstoke volunteered to take Charis and Frederica driving with him in the Park 'at the hour of the Grand Strut' to show the world that he was not a negligent guardian, and to discourage the pretensions of Charis' more persistent suitors. This was a handsome offer, as Alverstoke admitted that he rarely drove ladies. These drives were often an ideal time for private conversation. Mr Westruther took such an opportunity to quiz Kitty on her 'engagement' to Freddy in *Cotillion*. Jack Westruther had always been convinced that Kitty was his for the asking, and was rather piqued that matters weren't going the way he thought they should. He couldn't quite understand the game Kitty was playing.

There was a lovely scene set in the Park in *Arabella* when Mr Beaumaris was driving Arabella in his 'famous yellow-winged phaeton-and-four'. Like Jack Westruther, he too was intrigued by the behaviour of the lady with him. Arabella's brother, who was secretly visiting London to 'do' the town, had rented a 'showy chestnut hack' in order to parade with the best of them. A 'bruising rider', he knew that this was a part of society where he too could shine. Dismayed at encountering her brother while being driven around the Park, Arabella airily referred to him as an old friend, and Mr Beaumaris looked on with much amusement as Arabella tried covertly to convey to Bertram the need to be circumspect and not give away their origins.

Georgette Heyer's more spirited and extrovert heroines were often excellent whips and riders, and, to the horror of their male counterparts, could not be restrained from displaying their skill in public. Judith Taverner in *Regency Buck* was accustomed to being her own mistress. Despite her strong feeling of independence and her own large fortune, she had been forced to accept the guardianship of Lord Worth until she was to come of age. Nevertheless she was determined to make her mark in London and, with the approbation of Mr Brummell himself, she acquired a perch-phaeton. As so often happens in the novels, Lord Worth did not believe she was capable of driving such a potentially dangerous vehicle – they were the easiest of all carriages to overturn. Judith happily offered to take his own team of greys for a 'test drive' to prove her ability and, as Lord Worth discovered, 'She had fine, light hands, knew how to point her leaders, and . . . was sufficiently expert in the use of the whip.' Miss Taverner was soon a familiar figure in the Park, driving a 'splendid match pair of bays in a very smart sporting phaeton with double perches of swan-neck pattern'. She would have set a decided new fashion for such equipages but, as Georgette Heyer pointed out, few ladies indeed could drive one horse, let alone a pair, with anything like Miss Taverner's skill. On one of her dashes around the Park she was spotted by the Duke of Clarence, who had been rather taken by her. He requested to join her in the phaeton and she found she could converse with him quite easily, especially when she discovered that he had known the Admiral Nelson well.

Sophy's attempts to set up her own stable and to drive her choice of vehicle in the Park were far more fraught than Miss Taverner's, but then she had Mr Rivenhall, her cousin, to deal with; he was very much used to dictating to the rest of his family in an autocratic manner and assumed he could treat Sophy in the same fashion. The only way she could convince him that she was capable of driving something better than a horse 'quiet enough for a lady to drive' was to steal his team of greys while he was conducting some business in a street near St Paul's, and happily drive them around for half an hour.

Sophy eventually chose her own vehicle at a warehouse in Long Acre, helped in her decision by her cousins, Cecilia and Hubert, and the beautiful Endymion Fawnhope. Sophy finally bought a high-perch phaeton 'with huge hind wheels, and the body, which was hung directly over the front axle, fully five feet from the ground'. Endymion, with uncharacteristic vehemence, forbade his adored Cecilia from riding in it, not – as everyone at first thought – because he was concerned about her safety, but because it would destroy his vision of her as a 'porcelain nymph'. Much to Mr Rivenhall's intense anger, he soon had the pleasure of seeing Sophy driving her new equipage with 'Manningtree's match-geldings' in a very dashing, competent manner around the Park.

When Sophy really wanted to make Charles angry she deliberately took out

A high-perch Phaeton

his young blood chestnut in the tilbury. Even Sophy had trouble with this half-broken horse but at least she managed to prevent him bolting before Charles came to find her – which was her original intention.

Serena is another of Georgette Heyer's heroines who was an excellent whip and a strong character. As she said in *Bath Tangle*, 'The world began to talk about me when I drove a high-perch phaeton in Hyde Park.' She desperately missed the perfectly matched greys she used to drive here. They spoke about Venetia's mother in quite a different way in that novel. She put everyone 'to the blush' by driving a high-perch phaeton in the park every afternoon, drawn by four 'cream-coloured horses in blue and silver harness', which Sir Lambert had given her, but seemed a more appropriate gift for a mistress than a wife.

Sophy also had the gall to be an excellent rider and to own the beautiful, black Salamanca – definitely not an 'ideal horse for a lady' as Miss Wraxton rather cattily noted. Riding on the Row was considered acceptable exercise for ladies, but usually on a more suitable mount. Being new to England, Sophy was not familiar with all the rules governing riding in the Park, and she shocked the primmer visitors by going for a good gallop to 'shake the fidgets out of his legs'. Despite this faux pas, when she met the Countess Leiven, one of the formidable patronesses of Almack's, she was fortunate enough to be offered vouchers to enter the august institution. Such was Sophy's popularity that her dull, determined suitor Lord Bromford even bought a 'showy hack' so that he could ride up and down the Row every morning in the hope of meeting her here on Salamanca.

Miss Taverner, in *Regency Buck*, also rode a 'very spirited black', which became one of the sights to watch out for in the Park. Lady Serena, in *Bath Tangle*, was famous for her 'long-tailed grey', which she rode here regularly. When Sylvester (of the novel named after him) met Phoebe here in the Park, he saw that she was mounted on an animal 'with no paces and a placid disposition'. He offered to mount her on one of the horses he kept for his sister-in-law to ride, but Phoebe felt she could not accept this generous offer. The Duke was a clever man, however, so when he met his close friend Mrs Newbury he persuaded her to lend Phoebe her 'second hack', a non-existent animal that he would provide. Mrs Newbury had no objection to this scheme and invited Phoebe to go riding with her to Richmond, as she was longing for a good gallop.

Dysart, Nell's rakish brother in *April Lady*, was dashing enough to take the risk of riding a 'nervous young blood-chestnut' that most people would not have dared to exercise in the Park – at the fashionable time – when it was so crowded with traffic. While the hour between five and six was the most fashionable time to be seen in the Park, the more serious riders often exercised their horses here in the morning. Lord Charlbury was far more eligible than Lord Bromford, but even he expected women to be more fragile than men. He was extremely surprised to see Sophy riding Salamanca in the Park the morning following the Ombersleys' big ball. While discussing Lord Charlbury's chances of recapturing Cecilia's love, they were forced to gallop to avoid encountering Lord Bromford on his 'fat cob'. Many gentlemen in the novels came riding in the Park for exercise either before or after breakfast, like Lord Bridlington in *Arabella* who hence was not at home to deal immediately with the chimney sweep's boy whom Arabella had taken pity on.

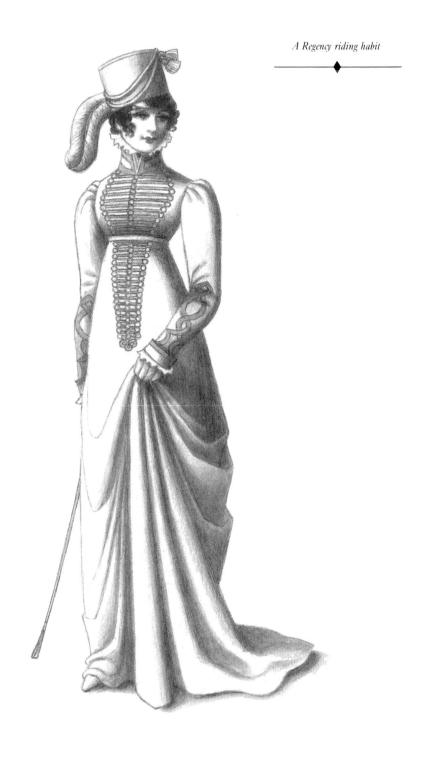

Balloon Ascents – Hyde Park, London

Walking in the Park was another favourite pastime, as it also combined the virtue of exercise and sociability. Kitty Charing in *Cotillion* invited Miss Broughty to go walking with her here to see how the daffodils and the crocuses were progressing. It was during this walk in the brisk spring air that Olivia confided to Kitty that she must marry well to save the family finances. Unfortunately the only man interested in such a legal union with Olivia was the ridiculous 'time-worn beau' Sir Henry Gosford, whom Olivia abominated. A far more eligible man like Jack Westruther was only willing to offer her a 'carte blanche'. But all was not lost, for they came upon the Chevalier, Kitty's cousin, who was being a 'gent du monde' and riding in the Park. He was not only able to solve their immediate predicament and tactfully get rid of the unwelcome attentions of Sir Henry but he and Olivia then stood gazing at one another: 'Never had there been a clearer case of love at first sight.'

Letty and Nell went walking in the Park before breakfast in *April Lady*. Upon their return, Nell was surprised to find her brother Dysart waiting for her, as he was not normally up before midday!

As you stroll in a westerly direction into the Park, and head up away from Rotten Row, you will come upon the Serpentine. Here, in winter, skating was to be had when the river was frozen over. Mr Rivenhall threatened to throw Sophy into the Serpentine if she dared try to ride his horse Thunderer. Since she'd already driven his greys without permission, he believed her capable of anything.

Various entertainments would be offered in the Park during the season, such as a re-enactment of the Battle of Trafalgar or a military review. Cardross ended up going solely with Letty to one of these reviews because Nell was so bowed down by her troubles that she had developed a persistent headache. The most unusual spectacles to attend were the balloon ascensions. The most exciting of these took place in the novel *Frederica*. In this book we met one of Georgette Heyer's most delightful young boys – the intrepid Felix, who was fascinated by anything to do with science. His friendliness and desire to learn, however, often led him into trouble.

With great ingenuity and charm, Felix persuaded his cousin Alverstoke to bring him to the ascension. While the Alverstokes sat in their carriage under the trees and socialized with the Merrivilles and Lord Buxted, Felix wandered off to get a closer view of the preparations for the ascent. Suddenly the peace of the scene was destroyed when the balloon started to rise into the sky with Felix clinging to one of the dangling ropes. As in all crises, everyone's true character came out. While Charis fainted, Jessamy turned white and Buxted stressed the danger, Alverstoke tried to keep everyone calm as the men in the balloon slowly managed to pull Felix inside. It was Frederica who persuaded Alverstoke to try to follow the balloon in his carriage, accompanied by a grateful Jessamy, and they headed out from the Stanhope Gate into the countryside, following the speck in the sky.

Walking on through Hyde Park you will come to Kensington Gardens. On one of her drives with Alverstoke during the fashionable hour, Charis confessed to him that she preferred Kensington Gardens because the flowers were so lovely there and it seemed more like the countryside. Later in the novel she arranged a surreptitious meeting with her beloved Endymion in this park to discuss what is to be done about their future. Both their families were against the match, and only her brother Harry supported her. While reviewing all the options open to them, and rejecting them all, Harry suddenly had a brainwave – it was *he*, not Frederica, who was Charis' actual guardian!

Green Park is a pretty, hilly, little park that also features in the novels. As you wander around, you will remember the chaos that the Merrivilles' huge mongrel dog Lufra caused when Charis and Frederica took him for a walk here. 'Undeterred by the Guide Book's tepid praise', they had come here in preference to Hyde Park, thinking it would be less crowded. Unfortunately the guidebook had failed to mention one of the most famous sights of the Park in those days – a herd of milch cows with milkmaids in appropriate costume ready, for a small sum, to dispense glasses of warm milk fresh from the cows. Lufra, who had already upset a family of young children with his desire to play, now saw a new challenge more fitting to his status. Before Frederica could stop him, he was among the cows, scattering them in all directions. Although not faint-hearted, Frederica was not able to soothe the cowman, the parkkeepers and the other interested busybodies, and she was obliged to lie and say that Lufra was a very rare breed of dog belonging to the Marquis of Alverstoke – to whose house they all trudged off.

Green Park was also the setting for a more serious scene in *April Lady*. Nell, unable to pay the bill for her court dress, had determined that the only course left open to her, as we have already seen, was to visit the moneylender Mr King. Using the ten percenters was seen as being bad enough for a man, but for a woman it was absolutely unthinkable. Nell stopped her carriage at the Bath Gate and sadly wandered through the Park, tossing about in her mind the ramifications of what she was going to do. Her thoughts were not happy ones as she realized that Mr King was not likely to lend money to a veiled lady who he didn't know. So it is with very heavy footsteps that she eventually headed across Piccadilly to Clarges Street.

It was at the same Bath Gate that Arabella, in a letter that she had sent by the Penny Post, asked her brother Bertram to meet her, as she couldn't possibly visit him at the Red Lion Inn where he was staying. Much to Arabella's distress, however, he didn't appear at the rendezvous, nor did he answer her note.

St James's Park is the least mentioned in the novels, but in *April Lady* Dysart had achieved temporary fame, of a kind, by cutting his initials on all the trees in an hour and fifteen minutes – a somewhat unorthodox way of enjoying the pleasures of the London parks.

The London parks, like London's architecture, have undergone some major face-lifts in the ensuing years since the Regency period, but with the flora the changes are not so strikingly obvious. The Regency spirit clings easily to the purlieu's of the parks and especially, the virtually abandoned, Rotten Row.

CHAPTER V

WHERE NOT TO LIVE:
The Fringes of Society

O ne doesn't have to read many of Georgette Heyer's Regency romances to realize that the 'ton' would only consider living in the most
exclusive area of London, which consisted of Mayfair and St James's.
The larger mansions were all in Mayfair, but single gentlemen often took up
lodgings in St James's, where they were close to their clubs and other male
preserves.

Characters in the novels who did not reside within these clearly defined
boundaries were stigmatized as living on the fringe of society, and would find it
extremely difficult to gain admittance to the elevated social heights that were a
prerequisite for all who belonged or wished to belong to the ton.

In order to be considered part of the ton – breeding was certainly an important
component, as well as address and manners; without the first two however,
fortune in itself was certainly of no avail. Added to these qualities was the
importance of living in the right place.

Mr Chawleigh in *A Civil Contract* was certainly a very 'warm' man, as the
wealthy were often referred to at that time. He had, however, made his money in
the City instead of inheriting it. Unlike many social aspirants in the novels, he
was not ashamed of his background and he'd bought a large, opulent mansion in
Russell Square because, as he said to Adam, 'You won't find me setting up in
Mayfair, all amongst the nobs.' Mr Chawleigh's social ambitions revolved purely
around his daughter Jenny. To that end he sent her to an exclusive ladies'

seminary in Kensington, and that was why he wanted her to marry Adam. Though Adam had inherited impoverished estates, he did have the title of Viscount Lynton. Just as good taste was, on the whole, seen to be a part of good breeding – although there are exceptions in the novels – the reverse was also true. Mr Chawleigh's house in Russell Square, which had been built on the site of the Old Bedford House, was a prime example of money run rampant. Adam, whose family home was the epitome of tattered stateliness, was somewhat taken aback by the dazzle of chandeliers 'mingled with yellow satin, gilded mirrors, chairs and picture-frames'. While the port was being passed after dinner, Mr Chawleigh happily spoke of all his possessions and the price he paid for them – much to Adam's discomfort. When Adam did marry Jenny, Mr Chawleigh typically, made it very plain that he wouldn't be expecting to visit them in Grosvenor Street and embarrassing Adam's family and friends.

The Merrivilles in *Frederica*, who were making a push to give the beautiful Charis one good London season, could only rent a house in Upper Wimpole Street. As the Marquis of Alverstoke said when he was requested to visit them, 'if my sister believes herself to be living quite out of the world in Grosvenor Place, what can one think of persons owning to Upper Wimpole Street?' As expected in such a location, the house turned out to bear the hallmarks of rented accommodation, being shabby and furnished inelegantly. Alverstoke discovered that he was not alone in this opinion, as Miss Merriville admitted, 'It is a horrid house, and not situated, as I've discovered, in the *modish* part of town.' Frederica had never been in London and had to rely upon the service of her Aunt Scrabster in order to find accommodation. As that lady herself lived in Harley Street, she saw nothing wrong with Upper Wimpole Street. Frederica was, however, dismayed to find herself living surrounded by people engaged in trade. On the other hand, Bernard Taverner of *Regency Buck* lived in Harley Street and from what she'd heard, Miss Taverner knew it 'to be a respectable neighbour-hood'.

Claud, the weak dandy in *The Unknown Ajax* suggested that Anthea and Hugo leave the matter of choosing a house to him, for he felt that they would otherwise end up 'in Russell Square, all amongst the Cits, those who worked in the city, and the bankers, or Upper Grosvenor Street, miles from anywhere'. Damerel jeered at Venetia's plans for setting up house alone with Aubrey in London. He thought she was far too beautiful to live outside society 'in Kensington, I think, genteel and retired! Or perhaps in the wilds of Upper Grosvenor Place, just on the fringe of fashion!' Even Mrs Hendred, Venetia's kind aunt couldn't approve of such a scheme and wouldn't have been more shocked if Venetia had wanted to enter a nunnery.

Despite everyone's disapproval of her plan, Venetia was determined to persevere with it, hoping that by being busy all the time she might in time come to forget Damerel. When she announced to Mrs Hendred that she had seen a house in Hans Town that she thought might be suitable for herself and Aubrey, that lady received the news with 'horrified incredulity' – whether at the thought of Venetia's projected life of spinsterhood or the 'deplorably dowdy locality' she had chosen, it is hard to tell.

The manipulative social climber Mrs Broughty admitted in *Cotillion* that she was staying in Hans Crescent 'quite out of the world', but it was not only her place of residence which made it difficult for her to break into the ton; she had neither birth nor good breeding to recommend her. Mrs Broughty had had no other recourse but to stay with her sister, Mrs Scorton, who was 'undeniably vulgar' and had of course 'no entree into the world of fashion'.

Hans Crescent and Hans Town were named after the famous botanist Hans Sloane. While the area was unfashionable in Regency times – one had to go through over a mile of countryside to get there – today it is one of the most exclusive areas of London, with the world-famous Harrods at its centre.

Kitty didn't realize quite how vulgar the Scortons were until she accepted an invitation to dine there. From the beginning of the evening, with Miss Scorton's prying questions about the exact nature of Lady Buckhaven's house, to the ill-advised outing to the masquerade at the Opera House later in the evening. Freddy, later in the novel, labelled Olivia Broughty's relations as a 'set of rum touches', and we can leave Hans Crescent with his parting shot in our ears: 'What's more,' he added, considering the matter dispassionately, 'not a good part of the town. Wouldn't like to live there myself.'

Hopping around town somewhat, but remaining within the same novel, Keppel Street, which is in Bloomsbury close to Russell Square, was not considered a good address either. This is where Hannah Plymstock, the beloved of the slow-minded Lord Dolphinton, lived. As Dolphinton says, his mother wouldn't have liked it and he didn't much either, especially as it was full of Cits. Despite these objections, Dolphinton braved his mother's censure and went there anyway, while everyone thought he was at Boodle's. Hannah lived there with her brother and his wife and children. Dolphinton didn't like her brother, not just because he was a Cit, but also because he was a Revolutionary and didn't want Hannah to marry an earl. It is in Keppel Street that Kitty first met Miss

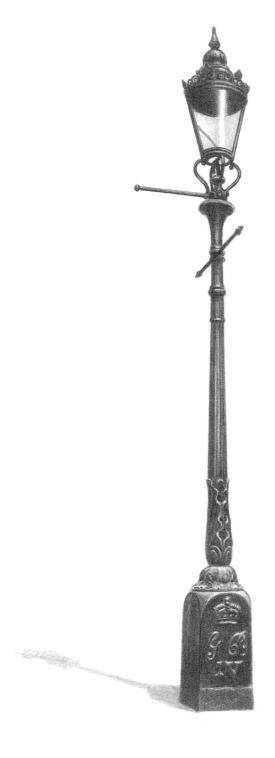

A lamp standard with the monogram of
King George IV

◆

Plymstock and, finding her to be stout, with sandy hair and lashes, was surprised that she could be the object of Dolphinton's love. She soon could see, however, that Hannah was very good for Dolphinton, as she was kind and sensible and treated him in a motherly way. More importantly for Dolphinton, as he said, Hannah had the kind of face he liked! When Lady Dolphinton spoke slightingly abut Grosvenor Place, Kitty wondered what she would have to say about unfashionable Keppel Street.

Lady Denville was convinced that once her sons were married it would be impossible to live with them. However, she vehemently stated 'I will *not* live in some dreadful, shabby-genteel quarter of the town, or miles and miles from anywhere, like Upper Grosvenor Place.' To demonstrate the kind of person who did reside in such a place we have Mr Jonas Steane in *Charity Girl* and according to Miss Henrietta Silverdale, 'There is bad blood in that family'.

Kensington was considered an acceptable place to go to school, but not a desirable place to live. Jenny, in *A Civil Contract*, attended a ladies' seminary there, her father hoping that it would thrust her into the ton. It didn't, but at school she became friendly with Julia, whose ethereal beauty led her to be known as 'The Sylph'. Unfortunately, Jenny's friend was also her husband Adam's first love, which caused Jenny many a secret pang; but publicly she dealt with the situation in her usual prosaic manner.

When Judith Taverner and her brother Sir Peregrine first arrived in London they were horrified to discover that the haughty man they had met on the road was their legal guardian. Judith informed him that she was going to ask one of her cousins, who lived in Kensington, to be her chaperone. Lord Worth coolly asked her what her purpose in coming to London was. When Judith replied that it was her goal to establish herself in the best circles, he unequivocally said, 'we need not consider the cousin living in Kensington'. Mrs Scattergood, who was Worth's choice for the role, confirmed this: 'A cousin in Kensington! You would find she would not add to your consequence.'

Out beyond Kensington is Chelsea. One afternoon when she had no more pressing engagement, Lady Cardross of *April Lady* drove out to the King's Road to visit Tubbs' Nursery garden in order to choose plants to decorate Cardross House for her grand ball. A novel idea at the time, she wanted to transform the ballroom into a 'fairyland of flowers', confident that this would give her ball supremacy that season and cause the other hostesses to 'gnash their teeth with envy'.

There were a few locales outside the purlieus of Mayfair where it seemed acceptable to live. Cavendish Square, just north of Oxford Street, was one of these. The Hendreds in *Venetia* invited Venetia to stay with them in Cavendish Square when her house 'Undershaw' was taken over by her new sister-in-law Charlotte and her unbearable mother Mrs Scorrier. Mrs Hendred, whose main aim in life was 'to remain in the forefront of fashion', would certainly not live anywhere that was not considered to be totally acceptable. Venetia, who had been given a room overlooking the Square, was told that she would find it far quieter than any looking out onto a street. After the quiet of the countryside, however, Venetia found London very noisy, with a seemingly ceaseless flow of traffic and the 'voice of the watchman, proclaiming the hour, and the state of the weather'. It was to Cavendish Square that Venetia's unwelcome suitor, Edward Yardley, was invited so many times to take 'pot luck' by Mrs Hendred, who hoped to promote the match.

In *Friday's Child*, the Honourable Ferdinand's parents also lived in Cavendish Square. Lord Worth was another notable resident. Judith and Peregrine Taverner, being new to London, had no idea where the Square was located but happily solved the problem by hiring a hackney to take them there. Lord Worth's residence turned out to be a large 'stucco-fronted house with an immense portico'. The evils of travelling in hackney coaches were brought home to the two of them when Peregrine had to remove a straw from his shoes before being sufficiently presentable to enter the house. Peregrine returned on a later occasion to ask for Worth's formal permission to become betrothed to Harriet Fairford. Despite the importance of his visit, which has caused him to arrive rather early, Peregrine is diverted both by the magnificence of Worth's bed with its bronze gryphons and crimson silk hangings, and also by Worth's successful creation of the *coup de vent* hairstyle which Peregrine himself had failed to achieve that morning. As readers will recall, the interview became rather unpleasant for Peregrine when Worth demanded payment of the IOUs he had won from him at the gaming tables.

Portland Place, just north of Cavendish Square, was also within 'the Pale'. The wilful but beautiful Tiffany Wield, in *The Nonesuch*, stayed here with her uncle, Henry Burford, who resided here in 'very good style', when she was in London. After three months Mrs Burford declared that they would 'be plunged into some shocking scandal' and she herself would 'dwindle into the grave' unless Tiffany left!

In order to get to Mayfair from Cavendish Square and Portland Place, one has to cross busy Oxford Street. Venetia, in her blue velvet and chinchilla outfit, went to the coach stand in Oxford Street to get a hackney. She looked so charming that 'the competition for her custom amongst the assembled Jehus was fierce, and extremely noisy'.

There are many other locations frequented, if not lived in, by Georgette Heyer's characters. Travel across to the Covent Garden area: when Lady Buckhaven in *Cotillion* learned that Kitty thought perfectly adequate dresses could be made at home, immediately suggested several linen-drapers in Leicester Square where they might purchase inexpensive material. Close by in Coventry Street, Bertram showed how youthful his tastes still were by visiting a peep show. Standing in the Haymarket, you can recall how Mr Rivenhall swept round the corner into this street, proving to his cousin Sophy, who was up beside him, that he knew 'how to drive to an inch'. It was also here that she saw August Farnhope and, pretending that he was an old acquaintance, persuaded Mr Rivenhall to pull up.

Long Acre, the street which runs north-east from Leicester Square, was the place where the characters came to buy their carriages. Peregrine Taverner came here with Mr Fitzjohn to look at a Tilbury, and this, of course, was where Sophy chose her infamous high-perch phaeton. On one of their few successful evenings together, Sophy and Mr Rivenhall had supper with the rest of their party in a fashionable hotel called The Star in Henrietta Street.

On the edge of Soho is Charing Cross. The Golden Cross Inn was the rendezvous appointed by Freddy in *Cotillion* to which he would bring Olivia Broughty in order for her and the Chevalier to elope together. Upon discovering, in the hack, that Olivia had not got a tooth- or hair-brush with her, Freddy bravely stopped at Newton's Emporium in Leicester Square to procure these items for her. Upon arriving in the yard of the Golden Cross, where the Chevalier was punctually waiting with a chaise, the two lovers fell into each other's arms. Freddy, who was somewhat embarrassed by this public display of passion witnessed by sundry waiters, explained it away by declaring incontrovertibly that they were 'French' before urging the pair on their way to Dover to catch the packet to Calais.

Adam's banker, the old firm of Drummonds, was in Charing Cross. They were a very 'old-established' bank who numbered among their clients no less a personage than His Majesty King George. Adam, who had a strong moral conscience regarding the debts he was left by his father, felt he should see Mr Drummond himself, rather than leaving it to his man of business. Mr Drummond, too, thought that personal service was in order, as the Deverils had been with the bank since its earliest days.

Moving east into the City, we venture into territory where the ton only resorted to for matters of business or in desperation. Louis de Castres, the mysterious Frenchman who was found murdered under a bush in Lincoln's Inn Fields, lived in a lodging near the Strand. It was not a very safe area, but apparently de Castres always scorned the escort of a link boy, and insisted on walking home alone. On a less sinister note, Lady Ombersley and Cecilia in *The Grand Sophy* visited a silk warehouse in the Strand.

Close by is where Somerset House is located, which is – as noted in previous chapters – where they held art exhibitions in the Regency period.

Just north of the Strand in Holborn Bertram, in *Arabella*, went to a menagerie and saw a badger being drawn – a cruel sport which had been declared illegal but could still be found in some undesirable neighbourhoods. Holborn was also the location of the Castle Tavern where the Honourable Ferdinand, in *Friday's Child*, spent such a pleasant evening with his friend Mr Ringwood that they decided to continue their libations at Ringwood's lodgings in Stratton Street. It was the excuse of an engagement in Holborn that made it so natural for Francis Cheviot to accompany home de Castres on the unfortunate evening that de Castres was murdered by Francis. The White Horse Inn, from which the Bristol coach left, was situated in Fetter Lane in Holborn. Pen, at the beginning of *The Corinthian*, begged Sir Richard Wyndham to tell her the way there so she could travel into Somersetshire and find her childhood friend Piers. Perceiving, in his inebriated state, how improper it would be for Miss Creed to travel on the stage by herself, Sir Richard agreed to accompany her.

East from Holborn, and just north of the City, is Broad Street. Behind here the Beggar's Club was located in a cellar in what was then slums. It was 'presided' over by the Earl of Barrymore, also known as Cripplegate. Barrymore's reputation was so bad that every young impressionable man who was tempted into his society was considered to be on a straight path to total ruin. The club, as Georgette Heyer says, was 'patronized by all the raff of town'. One of its unique features was that the members ate their suppers 'out of holes carved in the long table, and with knives and forks that were chained to their places'.

Closer to the river is Lombard Street, where the General Post Office was located. The Duke of Sale in *The Foundling*, having decided to live incognito for a while, travelled here to catch the mail coach. Having always travelled in a style befitting his rank, he was unfamiliar with the schedules and didn't realize that all the coaches travelled overnight and hence left London at eight-thirty in the evening. Undeterred by this state of affairs, he was directed on to the Saracen's Head in Aldgate High Street. At the busy coach office here he was successful in booking a 'box seat on the Highflyer', which left at eight in the morning. Venetia too dashed off to the General Post Office in Lombard Street when she felt that her reputation had been sufficiently tarnished by contact with her reprobate mother for her to present herself to Damerel. Her destination was York, but the coach was seriously delayed by fog in London and arrived in the North much later than it should have.

North from the City, Islington Spa was described in *Regency Buck* as a village. Elm trees grew on the Green, there was a pound for strayed cattle, and a scattering of coaching inns. In *The Corinthian*, the unromantic Melissa accused Sir Richard Wyndham of 'hobnobbing with the bourgeoisie at Islington Spa' when he said he would like to marry a woman who loved him.

Even further out is Golders Green where the poor Mrs Fitzherbert, the morganatic wife of the Prince Regent, had been banished to live – an unthinkable fate that put her beyond the reach of even the fringes of society.

CHAPTER VI

CULTURAL PURSUITS:
Edifying Sights and Occupations

In Georgette Heyer's novels it was considered an advantage to be witty – provided one did not go beyond what was considered 'pleasing'. Many of her heroines were distinguished by their quick minds and lively tongues, but again a line was always drawn, and too great a liveliness frowned upon. Mr Yardley in *Venetia*, for example, was constantly concerned that Venetia was too vivacious and outspoken, and that this would lead her into some indiscretion. On the other hand, some of the heroes – those classic Georgette Heyer creations who had reached their late thirties and were bored by all the pretty faces with no minds who had sent out lures to catch them – were captivated by the freshness and independence of the Judith Taverners, the Sophys, and the Serenas in the novels.

However 'clever' these more interesting heroines might be, it was certainly not acceptable for young ladies to be 'bookish'. Serena, in *Bath Tangle*, laughingly said that Fanny would make people think that she, Serena, was a blue stocking if she kept on about her cleverness. Serena felt slightly guilty, however, as she was very quick-witted and missed the company of like minds. Charlotte, Conway's new wife in *Venetia* seemed to be completely ruled by her mother and to lack any character of her own. With obvious alarum she had already asked Venetia if she was bookish – as if nothing could be more intimidating. At the other end of the spectrum, Ancilla's mother in *The Nonesuch* was considered to be 'very blue'. As the daughter of a professor of Greek she was able to save money by educating her remaining daughter herself – a task for which she was well-qualified. However, the dashing Sir Vincent Talgarth in *The Grand Sophy* said that 'blue-stockings . . . exercised a lowering effect upon his spirits,' and he carefully extricated Cecilia from the intellectual conversation of Mr Fawnhope and Miss Wraxton in the gardens at Merton.

There is a splendidly funny scene in *Lady of Quality* which illustrates how unfashionable it was to be bookish. Miss Annis Wychwood, having rescued the two young people, Lucilla and Ninian, when their carriage broke down, recommended the Pelican as a suitable, inexpensive inn for Ninian to put up at in Bath. As an added temptation, she mentioned that Dr Johnson slept there. Ninian was at sea and thought the gentleman in question must have been one of Miss Wychwood's relatives. When he discovered he was a 'writing cove', Ninian rather obviously admitted that he 'never had the least turn for scholarship'. He then overwhelmed Miss Wychwood by saying that 'no one would ever suspect' her of being bookish. Lucilla added her mite by betraying the fact that her hostess even 'keeps books in her bedchamber!' All of which amused Annis greatly.

Tom Orde, Phoebe's friend in *Sylvester*, found it hard to accept that his old playmate had actually written a novel which would be published. Realizing that he had offended Phoebe, he hastily explained himself by claiming that he wasn't 'bookish' and hence didn't know much about these things.

In *A Quiet Gentleman* Miss Morville explained to the Earl of St Erth that her family generally resided in London 'so that Mama may enjoy the benefits of literary society'. The Earl considered this rather dull, and Miss Morville agreed that it was very much so for those who were not inclined that way. She herself joined the society of her aunt, who chaperoned her to the theatre and all of the parties.

The young, lame Aubrey, in *Venetia* was, although only sixteen years old, one of Georgette Heyer's serious intellectuals. Clara Denny was quite intimidated by him, and referred to him as being 'very bookish'. She admitted that she didn't understand half the things Aubrey said, whereas the pedantic Edward apparently explained things most clearly.

Even though they might not have been 'bookish', many of the young ladies and gentlemen who came to London for the first time had a desire to see the more edifying sights. Harry, the eldest brother and hence head of the Merriville family in *Frederica*, complained, however, that when he was on his first visit to London he was dragged about 'to the stuffiest places'.

Venetia, 'who can converse as easily with a clever man as with a stupid one', liked to go off in the afternoon, in a hack by herself, to various places of interest in London. She enjoyed her independence and was quite happy to visit these places alone, despite the protests of Mrs Hendred, her aunt and hostess. She visited much the same places we would today – Westminster Abbey, the Tower of London, and the British Museum. Unlike Venetia, however, we don't have to worry about being thought of as a blue stocking. Part of Venetia's goal on these trips was to try to keep herself occupied and her mind off her love for the profligate Lord Damerel. Among the possible unexceptional suitors that her hostess picked out for her was a Mr Armyn, an expert on Roman remains. Mrs Hendred felt that he might have suited a young lady who spent three hours at a time in the British Museum and who read books on the Middle Ages!

With those new to the city, guidebooks were as popular then as today. The Miss Merrivilles relied on one in *Frederica*, and the pompous Edward Yardley slavishly followed one on his last trip to London, reading it from cover to cover again on the journey down 'to refresh his memory'. Kitty Charing in *Cotillion* could not have been considered at all intellectually inclined but, having been immersed in the depths of the countryside all her life, she was eager to see all the sights of the town and assumed that her cousin Freddy would escort her. He was horrified that she wanted to go to view these 'historic edifices' and was even more dismayed to discover that she had bought a comprehensive guidebook entitled *The Picture of London*. Even though Freddy wasn't academic by any means, he did however have a heart, as Kitty continually discovered. When she tearfully said she might never have another opportunity to come to the metropolis, Freddy capitulated and agreed to squire her.

It was not, however, a pleasant experience for him. At Westminster Abbey they took in everything, including the twelve chapels and Shakespeare's grave – until Freddy announced that he felt he was 'back at Eton'. The British Museum was their next port of call, but when Freddy discovered that the guidebook said they would have to spend at least three hours there, he managed to dissuade Kitty from her desire to tour the three departments of Manuscripts and Medals, Natural and Artificial Products, and Printed Books.

Young Felix in *Frederica* shared Freddy's feelings about the British Museum, saying that it contained a collection of 'fusty *old* things'. The only educational visit Felix and Jessamy made together in a week of unalloyed pleasure was to climb the three hundred and forty-five steps to the top of the Monument. On the iron balcony at the top, where they stood for sixpence each, Felix had the doubtful pleasure of hearing from Jessamy that it was higher than Trajan's Pillar by twenty-four feet.

Tom Orde, the Squire's son, who had come up to London to acquire a little 'town bronze' in the novel *Sylvester*, was excited at the prospect of finally seeing some of the places he' had heard about for so long – definitely not *'edifices'* but *'interesting'* places of a more masculine and adult appeal – like Jackson's Saloon, Cribb's Parlour, and the Fives Court.

Freddy was not spared the Elgin Marbles at Burlington House which had been shipped to England by Lord Elgin in 1803. Having paid the price of admission and bought a catalogue, he was flabbergasted to find 'they've got no heads!' and – what's more – no arms. Despite Kitty's attempts to interest him in art, Freddy was obdurate in thinking the whole thing a cheat.

Not discouraged, Kitty then relentlessly dragged him off to see St Paul's, Cornhill, the Bank of England, and the Royal Exchange. The guidebook saved the day and came to Freddy's aid by describing the above in rather disparaging terms. The weary sightseers could therefore head home to Berkeley Square with impunity.

Kitty was still full of enthusiasm, and the next day was ready to set out again. Having done their duty and seen the Guildhall, they then headed to the Tower and the New Mint. To his surprise, Freddy actually enjoyed himself.

They are no longer there today, but in the Regency period one of the major attractions at the Tower was the collection of wild beasts. The Tower was not the only place where they kept such an exhibition. One of the first things that Miss Judith Taverner and her brother Peregrine did when they arrived in London was to go to see the wild animals at the Exeter Exchange.

Charis and Frederica also had recourse to a pocket guide in the novel *Frederica*. They too were 'country-bred', and London was full of places to explore. Armed with their guide and carefully following its directions, they ranged across the town viewing 'edifices, monuments, and mansions', protected from unwanted attention by their enormous dog Lufra.

The famous Elgin Marbles appear again in *Arabella*. As soon as Mr Beaumaris returned to London after his surreptitious visit to the vicarage at Heythram, he went to Park Street to visit Arabella. He found that she had gone with Lady Bridlington and her son to visit the Marbles at the British Museum, where they were on show in a specially built wooden hut. He found her there, gazing intently at a 'sculptured slab from the Temple of Nike Apteros and being lectured to by the self-consequential Lord Bridlington. Lady Bridlington quickly perceived that a *tête à tête* between the two would-be lovers was in order and drew her son away. She even went so far as to invite Mr Beaumaris to accompany them to Somerset House to see the paintings there. Tactfully anxious to leave the interesting pair alone together again, she dragged her son off to see Sir Thomas Lawrence's latest work. It was amidst all this culture that Arabella shyly asked Mr Beaumaris if he still wanted to marry her. Arabella's motives were mixed. While she really did care for Mr Beaumaris, she also viewed marriage to him as the only way to solve her brother Bertram's pecuniary problems.

Other matches in the novels were promoted under the guise of absorbing culture. Kitty in *Cotillion* had taken to spending a great deal of time in Lord Dolphinton's company. Freddy, her supposed betrothed, viewed the matter complacently until he saw Miss Charing entering the Egyptian Hall with Dolphinton. The Egyptian Hall was the other name for Bullock's Museum, situated on the south side of Piccadilly, opposite Old Bond Street. It housed curiosities from the South Seas and from North and South America; a collection of armoury, and works of art; together with its latest acquisition, the travelling carriage of the Emperor Napoleon.

As Freddy discovered, when he arrived inside, Kitty was enjoying the exhibits by herself. So put out was Freddy that Kitty was obliged to reveal to him the real reason for her visits there with Lord Dolphinton – but only after Freddy had assured her that he wouldn't harm Dolph. Thus Freddy was able to meet Miss Plymstock and to become embroiled in Kitty's scheme to help the strange pair marry.

While being bookish was frowned upon, the novel *Sylvester* was interesting as the plot revolved around a heroine – the thin but interesting Phoebe Marlow, whose life was complicated enormously by a book she had actually *written*. Definitely not a dry treatise, it was a wickedly amusing novel, libellous by today's standards, utilizing and mocking many of the people she had met during her first season in London. The situation became fraught when she found herself being courted by Sylvester, the prototype for her wicked villain in the book. Attempts to suppress publication failed, and to her intense mortification she had the dubious felicity of seeing her novel become the talk of the ton. Of course all worked out happily in the end but when Phoebe suggested that she could restore Sylvester's reputation by writing another book making him the hero, he very firmly said 'no'. In this same novel, the most admirable woman, the Duke's mother, was also an author – of poetry – published by Mr Blackwell. Confined to a chair by a severe arthritic condition, she had had a special desk made to fit over it so that she could work in comfort. Although not exactly a secret, and despite anonymous publication, the Duchess' writing was something that she didn't talk about even with her closest friends.

Novel reading as an occupation for young ladies, or any ladies for that matter, was generally frowned upon as an unfit activity that would promote both moral and mental laxity. However, as we see in several of Georgette Heyer's novels, the reading of such fiction was too entertaining to be resisted. Phoebe first got her inspiration to write her own book from the many novels – acquired somewhat subversively through Miss Battery's subscription to a Bath lending library – she and her governess, Miss Battery, had enjoyed reading together.

Despite the pernicious effect of such reading, the heroines, when faced with a choice of action of crisis proportions, usually realized that, while some actions were acceptable in novels, they could not be condoned or executed in real life.

The Opera and the Theatre

It is a moot point in the novels whether or not to class visiting the opera and theatre as a cultural activity. While the characters often enjoy the productions they go to see, the greater import seems to be on the social interaction that takes place between the acts. Like promenading in the Park, visiting the theatre was another social pivot in the fashionable world.

Jack Westruther in *Cotillion* was playing a very cool game with Kitty Charing, but he did invite both Meg and her to go to Sadler's Wells with him to 'see the great Grimaldi in a revival of his very successful pantomime, *Mother Goose*'. His choice of entertainment was determined by what would appeal to Kitty, for such an evening would not normally even be considered by such fashionable ladies as Meg.

On his first night in London, Peregrine, in *Regency Buck*, left Judith at the hotel as she was tired, while he, 'agog with excitement', went to Covent Garden to see Kemble. He was much impressed by the theatre itself, and could enumerate for Judith the next day how many boxes there were and how plushly they were hung. He talked about the number of candles and the smartly dressed people. Judith was most amused, however, by the fact that he wasn't too sure what play he'd seen – though he *thought* it was *Othello*. Mr Bernard Taverner had the honour of escorting Judith to her first play, and much to Peregrine's disgust, she chose to go to a tragedy at Covent Garden. Upon another felicitous visit to Covent Garden, however, Peregrine was presented to the Fairfords by his friend Fritz. As his sister discovered, this meeting was to change his life as he immediately fell in love with Harriet Fairford. So struck was he that when Judith asked him to describe the young lady he had no clear recollection of her colouring!

Sophy, in *The Grand Sophy*, also wanted to see Kemble act. In a rare moment of accord, her cousin, the autocratic Mr Rivenhall, engaged a box at Covent Garden and took her there one evening with Cecilia and Mr Wychbold. He, however, thought the great actor affected, and his odd pronunciations distract-

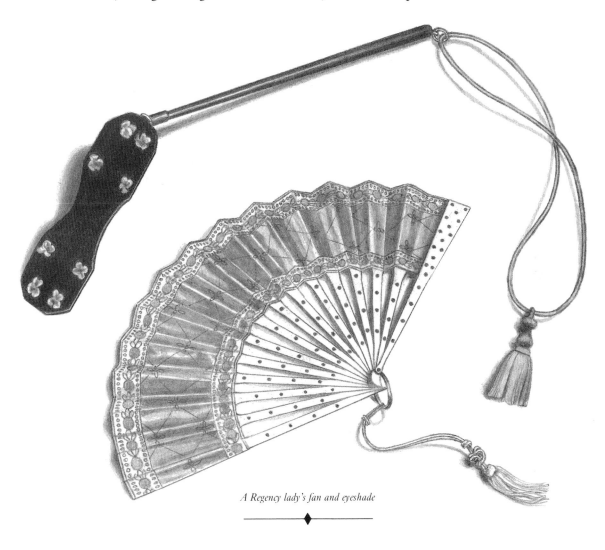

A Regency lady's fan and eyeshade

ing. The evening was still a great success – only rivalled by Lord Charlbury's theatre party to Drury Lane to see Kean, another famous actor, in the play *Bertram*.

In *A Civil Contract*, Lydia, while visiting Jenny in London, fell in love with the theatre after only one visit to Drury Lane where she saw *Hamlet* played by Kean. She was so impressed by this actor that she could not bear to stay and see the farce. Letty watched him in two more plays, and her one ambition in life was to play opposite him – despite the fact that she was 'half a head taller' than he was and her bent was for comedy rather than tragedy.

In the novel *The Covenient Marriage*, Nell agreed to go with Letty and Cardross to Drury Lane in order to prevent Letty from teasing Cardross into letting her marry Allandale. The play was mediocre, however, and they all agreed to leave early. Apparently London was going through a 'dramatic doldrums'. The Haymarket Theatre had been closed and the Surrey Theatre on the South Bank was only producing burlettas, 'not at all the thing for ladies'. The Lyceum and the Olympia were putting on shows that were more akin to the type of entertainment found at Astley's, so that only left Drury Lane and the San Pareil, where a 'succession of indifferent plays' was available. Drury Lane, after being burnt down, opened again in 1812. Its domed Corinthian rotunda is the only remaining example of an interior of a Regency theatre in London.

Unfortunately, it was not the opera season while Venetia was in London, but a visit to the theatre changed her life. Edward Yardley, her boring suitor from home, invited Venetia and her hostess, Mrs Hendred, to a select dinner at the Clarendon Hotel followed by a trip to the theatre. Venetia was absent-minded all evening, tossing plans around in her head 'for achieving social ruin'. While Venetia suffered this contemplative state, the play went by in a haze until the end of the first act, when she noticed a very beautiful but scantily dressed older woman in the box opposite. The woman half-acknowledged Venetia, but when she asked Mrs Hendred the woman's identity Mrs Hendred started to feel faint and had to leave the theatre. High drama! Later, in the midst of her spasms, Mrs Hendred, with the help of Edward Yardley, managed to tell Venetia the true story of her mother and Venetia immediately saw the answer to her problem.

Very few of the characters seemed to attend the opera in the novels, and many of them were professedly unmusical. In *A Civil Contract*, Adam, who had had to marry for money but was very proud, was surprised to learn that he and his wife Jenny had rented a box at the Opera House. Because Adam was always sensitive about accepting gifts from her father, Mr Chawleigh, Jenny was embarrassed to admit that the box was a present to her because her father knew her to be fond of music. Adam immediately felt uncomfortable for he had not thought to provide a box for Jenny himself – adding that hers would be above his touch as it must have cost at least four hundred guineas. Jenny had sufficiently overcome her social shyness to invite Brough's family, the Adversanes, to go to *Alceste* with her while Adam was away. When Jenny took Lydia to the Opera, they had a very exciting evening as they were witnesses to the public rivalry between the Regent and his Princess. He was seated in the royal box, flanked by the Tsar and the King of Prussia. The Princess, who had been 'excluded from participation in any of the royal festivities', took her revenge by sweeping into the box opposite the Regent's while 'God Save the King' was being sung.

As we have seen, the characters were always likely to see people they knew, both at the theatre and the opera, as the ton represented a small fraction of the population and they all patronized the same venues. Lighthearted enjoyment was the keynote of their lives, and if this enjoyment could be spiced with wit, so much the better.

CHAPTER VII

PLEASURE JAUNTS:
Escaping From the Heart of London

E ven with its refreshing spans of green parks, London of the Regency period was, as it is now, a noisy, bustling place – crowded with people and carriages. Members of the ton enjoyed escaping out of it on driving or riding excursions, for a brief respite.

One of the favourite places to which one could drive or ride was Richmond Park. The park had originally been created by King Charles I who wished to have a hunting preserve close to London. Public access to the Richmond Park was a continuing bone of contention until the late eighteenth century when cardboard tickets authorizing entrance to carriages became available. If you go there today you will understand why this parkland was such a popular destination. With its expansive vistas of natural, open green, it provides now, as it did then, miles of paths to walk and ride on in as you would the true countryside.

Sylvester agreed to escort Phoebe Marlow and his cousin Mrs Newbury to Richmond Park on the 'first real spring day' as they were 'pining' for a good gallop which was, of course, forbidden in Hyde Park. Richmond Park was also the closest place to Mayfair where horses could really be exercised. When the day for the expedition arrived, the party had been enlarged to include Major Newbury, Sylvester's sister-in-law Ianthe and, much to Sylvester's annoyance, her suitor Sir Nugent Fotherby – that veritable 'sprig of fashion'. Despite Ianthe's reputation for being late, they all met in good time at the Roehampton Gate and proceeded to enjoy the Park. Phoebe thought that Sir Nugent looked like a 'coxcomb', 'padded in at the waist, exaggeratedly padded at the shoulders' and, 'everything he wore seemed to have been chosen for the purpose of making him conspicuous'. Not only was his appearance ridiculous but even Ianthe had to admit that he was quite 'addle-brained'. Sir Nugent's pedigree was excellent however, and his income of at least £60,000 a year obviously blinded Ianthe to a number of his faults. While awful civilities were being exchanged between this ill-assorted company, they did manage to enjoy a few good gallops: Phoebe on her lovely new mare, Firefly, which Sylvester had cunningly managed to provide for her on the pretence of it being Mrs Newbury's second hack.

On the pretext of wishing to talk to her about the sweep's boy Jemmy, Mr Beaumaris lured Arabella (in the novel named after her) out for a drive to Richmond Park. Arabella had proved so elusive that he was obliged to employ such an 'ignoble stratagem' in order to see her. It was such a sunny afternoon that Arabella decided to wear a fetching straw hat and to take her new parasol, and as they drove down in Beaumaris' curricle Arabella confided to him that she loved going to Richmond Park as it was like being deep in the countryside. It was such a fine dry day that they decided to stroll for a while in the Park, while the groom took care of the carriage. Conversing all the time, Mr Beaumaris subtly tried to discover more about Arabella's mysterious background. She, however, immediately resumed her society manner and did not give him the benefit of her confidence, but instead 'became interested in the countryside'.

Mr Westruther in *Cotillion* also took advantage of a glorious sunny day to invite Kitty Charing for a drive to Richmond Park to see the primroses. Jack Westruther, who was tired of Kitty's sham betrothal to Freddy and felt it was time to act and assert his own claims on her, saw a trip to Richmond Park as an ideal opportunity. To ensure further that they would be completely alone together, he did not bring his Tiger with him (the small boy with whom it was traditional to drive out), saying that as they were cousins such chaperonage was quite unnecessary! Like Arabella, Kitty was emboldened by the fine weather 'to wear a Villager-hat of satin straw, with flowers at one side, and an apple-green ribbon'. A far cry from the plainly garbed Kitty of before, Jack could find no quarrel with her appearance. His behaviour was quite unexceptional throughout the entire outing; he even forbore laughing at Freddy, and Kitty spent a very pleasant afternoon in his company. A masterful flirt, he left her at the end of the day calling her his 'foolish, doubting little Kitty', which caused her to blush rosily at this tribute from her childhood hero.

Jack, as we know, was playing a double game and was also pursuing the frail blonde beauty Miss Broughty, though his intentions in this quarter were not at all honourable. When he called at the Broughty home in Hans Crescent to invite Olivia to drive with him to Richmond he was not as lucky as his rival, the debonair Chevalier, who was already ensconced there, and Jack had to abandon his plans for the expedition.

Richmond Park was also a favourite destination for gentlemen who wished to try out their new horses. In *Frederica* the Marquis of Alverstoke was planning to drive to the park to judge the paces of a 'team of high-bred greys, warranted by their late owner to be sweet-goers'. His plans were disrupted by the arrival of Jessamy and Felix. Felix was determined to hold Alverstoke to his promise to visit the Soho Foundry and could not be swayed from that scheme – even by the offer of a drive to Richmond with the Marquis. Jessamy, who was horse-mad, thought his brother was a clodpole, but Felix, as usual, got his own way. Meanwhile Jessamy was thrilled to be allowed to see the greys and even had a quick spin round the square with them. Such was his enthusiasm that Alverstoke found himself offering to take Jessamy along on his next trip to the Park to try them out – an invitation which left Jessamy delirious with happiness. The trip, when it happened, was everything he dreamed it would be. Alverstoke not only had tickets of admission to the Park, but he even allowed Jessamy to handle the reins for a while, and showed him 'how to turn a corner in style . . . and how to point the leaders'.

Lord Wrotham also planned to 'tool down to Richmond' when he visited Sherry the morning after Hero left her husband. He professed that he wanted to take her with him to try out his new team – 'Prime bits of blood!' It was all a hoax to worry Sherry, for Wrotham knew full well that Hero was not there.

On a more whimsical note, Altringham in *Arabella* came down to Richmond Park to root up a bunch of dandelions so that he could plant them in his window-box and have plenty on hand to wear in his button-hole. Altringham was foolishly aping Mr Beaumaris who had decided to start this new fashion as a joke. Richmond was also a favourite place for *al fresco* parties. Nell used Lady Brixworth's planned event in the park as an excuse to escape from her husband Cardross when he started pointing out that he never saw her any more. Nell, who loved him but had been avoiding him because of her debts, pleaded that she must dash off and get ready as Letty was waiting for her.

Another popular, out-of-town destination was Wimbledon, not so much for pleasure but more often a case of duty, as various characters had relations living there. The Dowager Duchess of Wigan, Mr Beaumaris's grandmother, was a resident, and it was she who he visited when he was at a loss as to what to do about Arabella. His journey was enlivened by the company of the mongrel Ulysses who refused to be left behind and ran panting after the curricle until Mr Beaumaris took pity on him and allowed him up beside him. It was to the Duchess's house in Wimbledon that he eventually took Arabella when she thought they were eloping to Gretna Green together. Arabella was surprised at how short the first stage of their journey was, but as it was late at night it was not until she was in the large house and was handed a glass of milk by the housekeeper, that she realized that she had not been a participant in a traditional elopement!

Poor Mr Allandale also had recourse to Wimbledon in *April Lady* when Letty, his tempestuous love, persuaded him that he must elope with her. Letty had got her way by having a fit of hysterics in Allandale's lodging, but no matter how put upon, Allandale was too proper to countenance anything such as a runaway match. He, too, cunningly convinced Letty that they were off to the Broder but, in fact, he took her to his mother's house in Wimbledon.

In Regency England, Hampton Court was as popular a place to visit as it is today. While many people now choose to go there by water – a somewhat long trip on the winding Thames – in the novel *Frederica* they decided to drive. As part of his new role as unofficial guardian to the Merrivilles, the Marquis of Alverstoke found himself inveigled into the unusual position of agreeing to participate in this family party. As a further test of his dignity, they all travelled in his barouche 'with its high-stepping horses, so very well-known to the members of the Four-Horse Club'.

The maze was the most popular attraction for the younger members of the family, but Alverstoke had providentially provided himself with a key to it. After impressing Frederica with his skill in solving its riddle he was able to extricate her from it, and sit and chat amiably while the others continued to be thwarted by its twists and turns. Today the intrepid explorer in the maze has to manage alone but then they had, as Georgette Heyer says, a 'custodian, whose stand commanded a view of the whole labyrinth, and whose duty it was to direct exhausted persons out of it'. Needless to say the energetic Merrivilles scorned such help.

Vauxhall is hardly outside London but as visitors had to go by boat to these pleasure gardens I have decided to include it in this section. Unfortunately, if

A Regency debutante in evening dress

you go to Vauxhall today you will find it a mess of railway lines; but even so, on looking at it from the northern side of the river it is pleasant to reminisce about the fairy-tale environment it once was.

It was from a gala night at the Vauxhall Gardens that Arabella and Mr Beaumaris decided to make their elopement together – Mr Beaumaris having promised to acquire all the necessities that would be required for a lady who was planning to be away overnight. He also said that he would have his coach ready and waiting by the Gardens so that they would be able to slip away unobtrusively. Arabella wished that her first visit to the Gardens could be under different circumstances, because her enjoyment was impaired by the momentous step she was about to take.

Approached by the river and entered through the water-gate, the Vauxhall Gardens certainly did resemble a fairyland. They were lit by thousands of lamps which illuminated the groves and the colonnades. A number of attractions were provided for visitors. In the centre was a 'giant kiosk, glittering all over with coloured lights', which housed the orchestras; in a rotunda concerts were given; and there was a large mirror-lined pavilion where those who had not hired a private box could partake of supper. Fountains played and those with amorous intentions could dally along the many secluded walks.

Despite her troubles, Arabella was entranced by the 'Grand Cascade'; this consisted of a miniature moat, where water actually ran down a cascade and water mill, causing the vehicles to move in a lifelike manner – in the Rotunda. Well-to-do visitors such as Mr Beaumaris usually hired a box for their party, and it was traditional to nibble the wafer-thin shavings of ham that the Garden was famous for, and to drink rack punch. Firework displays were also part of the entertainment provided, and it was during such a show that Mr Beaumaris suggested they should slip away.

Sherry, in one of his moods of uxorial responsibility, put together a party of people to accompany Hero and himself to another Grand Gala night at the gardens. Isabella, 'The Incomparable', and her slavish admirer Lord Wrotham were included, and all went well until George's rival, the Duke of Severn, intruded upon their party, causing Wrotham to have a 'fit of the sullens'.

Tiffany Wield in *The Nonesuch* was wild enough to 'attend a masquerade at Vauxhall Gardens, escorted by a besotted youth'. It was bad enough not to be chaperoned but Tiffany was not even 'out' and it was this escapade that finally convinced Mrs Burford that Tiffany had to go.

The Taverners too partook of the classic fare at Vauxhall, Peregrine mixing the burnt wine with copious amounts of rack punch. They had been lucky enough to see 'Mr Blackmore performing feats on a slackrope', as well as the other usual attractions.

As we can see from the novels, society was in many ways restricted, and the number of places the ton would consider patronizing, extremely select. The characters, however, never seemed bored, and their days were filled with rounds of gaiety, as much out of town as in.

CHAPTER VIII

YOUTHFUL DELIGHTS:
Diversions for the Young and Unsophisticated

Oone of the many elements that lifts Georgette Heyer's novels far above the level of pure romances is the wide variety of characters she introduces into them. The innkeepers, grooms, abigails, and other servants often come alive in the same way that the members of the ton do. Part of this distinctive element is the wide age range in the novels. They are not just full of people of marriageable age but are also replete with the very old and the very young. Some of the most lively novels are those in which we encounter precocious youths who not only amuse us but often cause chaos in the lives of their elders.

In the Regency period London offered a large number of strange and unusual entertainments for those who were not yet old enough to participate in more adult pleasures. Obviously most of these 'treats' do not exist today, but it is interesting to review how the young people spent their time.

Astley's Amphitheatre was a favourite for the less sophisticated. Established in 1768 as a riding school and royal circus by ex-Sergeant-Major Philip Astley, it was beleaguered by fire but rebuilt in 1804. Referred to as the 'handsomest pleasure haunt in London', the interior was a cross between a theatre and a circus. It had a ring of sawdust and an orchestra pit that separated it from the classic proscenium arch and the largest stage in London. The whole area was lit by an enormous chandelier which consisted of fifty patent lamps. Looking at contemporary pictures of Astley's, with its lushly decorated interior, it is hard to believe that the exterior was constructed of ships' masts and spars, with a canvas ceiling – like our big tops today – supported by fir poles which had been lashed together by ropes. Readers will know that spectacular equestrian displays were the focal point of the entertainments at Astley's; these were performed by Astley's son, John, and Hannah, his daughter-in-law.

Sherry took his young bride Hero to Astley's to see a 'spectacular piece entitled Make Way for Liberty or The Flight of the Saracens'. Hero was thoroughly entranced by this performance and even Sherry, who was more blasé, enjoyed it more than he thought he would. Kitty, in *Cotillion*, was deprived of the pleasure of visiting this establishment and seeing the 'Grand Spectacles, and Equestrian Displays'. She was in London too early in the year, for it never opened its doors before Easter Monday.

Arabella's brother, Bertram, who had just been up to Oxford to take Smalls, felt that he deserved a holiday. Fortuitously, he met his friend Mr Scunthorpe, who was 'at home to a peg in London', so without his father's knowledge Bertram decided to 'do' the town. One of the more 'innocuous' places he visited was Astley's. Despite being a notable Corinthian, Sir Gareth Ludlow was not at all 'toplofty' and was extremely popular with his nieces and nephews. With the younger ones he achieved everlasting favour by taking them to such 'dizzy delights' as Astley's.

Endymion Daventry, the senior by several years, would on occasion take his two younger sisters to Astley's Royal Amphitheatre in the novel *Frederica*. Older brothers could often be relied upon for this treat. Mr Rivenhall took his three younger sisters to Astley's and it was here that they thought Amabel contracted the severe fever that endangered her life. Before her sojourn in Bath with Miss Wychwood, the only theatre Lucilla had ever seen was during a trip to Astley's when she was six years old.

The Duke of Sale, who in *The Foundling* was going under the pseudonym of Mr Rufford, bribed his young charge Tom with the promise of visits to Astley's Amphitheatre, the Royal Exchange and the wax effigies at Madame Tussaud's if he behaved himself until they reached London. Tom was most indignant that all he saw was St Paul's Cathedral the last time he was in London.

The wild beasts in the Tower were another favourite sight to visit. In *Arabella*, Freddy, on his mammoth tour around London, found this one of the more diverting places he had been forced to visit. Mr Ringwood in *Friday's Child* very cleverly chose to entertain Hero after lunch by taking her to see the wild beasts at the Royal Exchange – 'Nothing could have appealed more strongly to Miss Wantage's youthful taste'. Even Miss Taverner and her brother Peregrine made a trip to see the wild beasts as one of the first events on their city itinerary. The second day of Freddy's tour around London was also enlivened by a visit to the New Mint, where he and Kitty were actually allowed to watch the stamping of the coins – a process which Freddy found quite fascinating. Felix, in *Frederica*, was also eager to visit the New Mint with its gas-lighting and 'steam-engines of *vast* power' (not unexpectedly given his scientific bent). Unfortunately Felix discovered that no one could get in without a special recommendation, and he proceeded to importune his 'Cousin' Alverstoke both to write to apply and also accompany him there. Alverstoke, who had already been surprisingly altruistic with the boys, decided that he had had enough 'treats' and that his secretary Charles Trevor should go in his place.

The wax effigies at Madame Tussaud's were a prime favourite and, although not on the same site, this is still one of the premier stops for tourists to London. They were originally exhibited in the Strand and then moved to Baker Street. The two intrepid boys of *Frederica*, Jessamy and Felix, enjoyed the waxworks, but Kitty Charing was again out of luck – the exhibition was touring the country while she was in London.

Felix and Jessamy, although very different in character, shared a taste for the unusual. At only twelve, Felix had an interest in science that was intense beyond his years. With his impish, guileless countenance he managed to persuade the boys' reluctant 'guardian' Lord Alverstoke to take him to the Soho foundry in Wardour Street to see the pneumatic lift. The foundry was actually in Birmingham; this was one of the few times that Georgette Heyer made a mistake!

Lord Alverstoke was bemused to find himself agreeing to such an expedition and his friends, whom he encountered en route, were nonplussed at his new interest. Felix was also full of his visit to Merlin's Mechanical Museum where admission cost him half a crown. Felix was entranced most of all by such exhibits as the hydraulic vase, the mechanical cruising fingate, and a band of mechanical music. Not quite so impressive but also entertaining were the Antique Whispering Busts and an aerial cavalcade. Stimulated by these marvels, he planned next to go to the exhibition of Maillardet's Automaton at the Spring Gardens. Maillardet's Automaton was apparently 'a musical lady, who was advertised, rather alarmingly, to perform most of the functions of animal life'.

Felix with Jessamy also enjoyed such other attractions as the Exeter 'Change in the Strand', with its lions and tigers and 'an aquatic representation of Sadlers

A pedestrian curricle

◆

Wells'. One of the 'scientific' sights in London which Felix arrived too late to see was Trevithick's Locomotive. Trevithick had put this on show in Fitzroy Square on a piece of ground that he had fenced and laid a track on. Alverstoke told Felix that many people went to see it but few could be persuaded to take a ride in the attached carriage, especially after one of the rails broke and the engine was overturned.

The two of them also decided to visit the infamous Peerless Pool. This bathing place assumed an added lure in their eyes as it had formerly been known as the Perilous Pond, because of the number of people who had been drowned while swimming there. Situated in Moorfields, it had been made a perfectly safe place for bathing by the time of the boys' visit. It was springtime, however, and the day was so chilly that the temptation to dive into the water was deferred until warmer weather. Hero, in *Friday's Child*, was also tempted to visit the Peerless Pool, but luckily Sherry discovered her plans and was able to prevent her committing such a breach of ton.

Jessamy, bound to his self-imposed studies for a part of each day, chaffed at the lack of exercise available to him in London. In a mood of frustration, he discovered one of the latest rages in town – the Pedestrian Curricle! This apparently 'consisted of two wheels, with a saddle hung between them'. The rider would sit on this machine and use his feet to move forward, raising them and coasting when a decent speed had been attained. Such was Jessamy's enthusiasm, that he even took lessons before feeling bold enough to hire a machine and embark upon trial runs in the quieter streets, accompanied by Lufra the dog. Unfortunately, Lufra was his undoing on the day he decided to go for a final test run before exhibiting his new prowess to his family. Piccadilly was far more crowded than the streets he normally 'rode' on, and when Lufra had an altercation with a retriever he suspected of attacking Jessamy, total chaos reigned – with pedestrians, coaches and dogs all getting caught in the mêlée.

Arabella was very concerned that her brother Bertram had come to London without permission from their parents, especially as he looked so much older with a 'sophisticated waistcoat' and his hair brushed into a different style. She was relieved to hear the innocuous list of places he meant to visit, particularly when she heard how much he enjoyed a peep-show which he saw in Coventry Street, and that he was also keen 'to witness that grand spectacle *The Burning of Moscow*'.

Lydia in *A Civil Contract* had a superb time whilst she was in London – Mr Chawleigh had promised to show her all the sights, including the New Mint. Jenny has also volunteered to take her to Russell Square so that she could see the Cossack who stood outside the door of Mr Lawrence's studio while the Tsar was inside having his portrait painted. Jenny doesn't think it fair that Lydia be sent back to Bath before she had seen the Grand Spectacle in the Parks. This was to consist of a balloon ascent in Green Park, the battle of Trafalgar to be fought on the Serpentine, the Temple of Concord, and the Chinese Pagoda.

Shopping, then as now, was one of the most appealing aspects of the metropolis for young ladies, and Phoebe Marlow in *Sylvester* put off the selection of her own fashionable wardrobe so that she could not only take Alice – the innkeeper's daughter from the depths of the countryside – to see the most prominent sights of London, but also to that haven of bargain shopping: the Pantheon Bazaar.

With sights such as these, it is not surprising that the young people in the novels enjoyed themselves as much as their elders.

CHAPTER IX

DUELLING:
A Gentleman's Prerogative

Duelling had been outlawed in Regency England but, if provocation was given, no man would hesitate to settle the matter in the time-honoured fashion. As we can see from the following examples in the novels, the characters did not shirk from a fight, and some of the more youthful, volatile men would look for a duel on the slightest pretext – often after consuming large quantities of alcohol.

The etiquette surrounding duelling was strict. Engaging with anyone under age or where a great disparity existed was not a part of the code of honour. A prime example of this occurred in *Venetia*. Venetia's two permanent suitors, the stolid Edward Yardley and the mooncalf Oswald Denny, both resented the appearance of the rake Damerel in their territory. Oswald dreamed of a more noble time when all he would have to do to justify calling a man out would be to 'jostle' him in a doorway! It was Oswald, however, whose romantic daydreams led him to embarrass Venetia with unwanted passion until he was summarily picked up by the collar and thrown into the yard by Damerel who happened to be nearby. Incensed by such treatment, Oswald felt bound to challenge his rival. Damerel hoped that he was only speaking in the passion of the moment, but riding home he came upon Oswald barring the way across the lane. The young Denny had already regretted his rash words, but one of the rules governing a gentleman's behaviour in such situations was that once a challenge had been issued it could not be retracted. The last thing Oswald wanted was to be thought a coward. Damerel feels sorry for the young lad and understood how he felt but, as he pointed out to Oswald, it would be grossly improper for him to accept his challenge as he was old enough to be Oswald's father.

As we saw in *The Quiet Gentleman*, it was also grossly improper for a guest to call his host out or vice versa. Lord Ulverston, who was staying at Stanyon Castle, laughingly said that he meant to call out his old friend and host, Gervase, Seventh Earl of St Erth, in the morning after finding the exquisite Miss Bolderwood on his friend's arm when it was time for his own dance with her. A far more serious challenge took place later in this novel, again caused by Miss Bolderwood. When St Erth's younger half-brother Martin continued to press his attentions on Marianne in the greenhouse at her father's home, he seemed impervious to how much he was both hurting and frightening her. When her betrothed – Ulverston – came upon the scene, Martin transferred his rage to him. Ulverston was ready for the blow and in turn managed to floor Martin. Martin was furious and called Ulverston out, which Ulverston said was an impossibility as he was a guest in his brother's house. Martin, however, had lost all sense of reality and clinched the matter by striking Ulverston 'an open-handed blow across the cheek'. Such outright provocation could not be ignored, and Ulverston was determined to teach Martin a lesson.

The two, however, could not be allowed to meet – the impropriety would be too great and the ensuing scandal difficult to live down. A man of Martin's temper was not easily assuaged, and it wasn't until his brother the Earl informed him of the secret betrothal between Ulverston and Marianne that the duel could be avoided. The whole affair was very irregular: Martin was not only much younger than Ulverston but he was also his surrogate host. And as Gervase pointed out, the hot-tempered Martin was a superb shot and if he meant to force an encounter with Ulverston, which seemed likely in view of his mood, he would shoot to kill.

The Code of Honour also stated that the first duty of seconds was to try and bring about a reconciliation. Mr Warboys, in the above mentioned novel, was not exactly articulate but he laboured painstakingly over an epistle to achieve this end. Hester, in *Sprig Muslin*, was worried that Sir Gareth Ludlow would feel obliged to call out Mr Theale because he had run off with Amanda. Hester said it would be far more 'comfortable' if he did not! Sir Gareth thought this understatement extremely funny but he reassured her by saying that as Mr Theale was so old and fat he wouldn't even feel able to 'draw his cork'.

When reading the novels it is important to remember that in Regency times

London was much smaller than it is today, and many of the places that we now regard as being an integral part of the city were then individual villages located in the countryside, or large tracts of common land. As you travel around London, only the names will give you a clue to their previous rural history, for example, Westbourne Green and Chalk Farm. When a challenge was delivered in London, it was customary for the respective parties to meet on one of the greens or commons surrounding the heart of town.

Even Beau Brummell, a most pacific man, had been called out once, and was due to meet his opponent at Chalk Farm. In *Regency Buck* he told the story to an amused group at Watier's. Wittily, he relayed his sleepless night beforehand and how his fear had increased when his Second recited all the necessary details of what would happen. Determined, however, to see it through, he arrived at the appointed time on the ground where 'each minute seemed an age, as in terror and semi-suffocation', he awaited the other party's approach. The minutes ticked by and finally after a full hour his Second announced, to his profound relief, that they could now honourably depart.

In the same book, Peregrine was also saved at the last minute but under completely different circumstances. There was something suspicious about Peregrine's duel with Farnaby right from the start. First of all, Peregrine was a minor and as we have already discussed, no true gentleman would thus engage him in such an affair. Farnaby was also not regarded as a member of the ton; in fact his background seemed rather shady. Finally, Peregrine was actually provoked by Farnaby into punching at a cockpit when Farnaby accused Peregrine of having his bird 'pressed' to make him fight.

Another rule in the Code of Honour was that no apology could be extended or received after a blow. Westbourne Green near Paddington was the appointed place for this engagement. At only nineteen, Peregrine faced his first duel. He was exceeedingly nervous but made a laudable attempt to appear plucky, as his Second, Mr Fitzjohn, was proud to see. It is hard to imagine Westbourne Green as a tiny hamlet surrounded by fields, but we can shudder with Peregrine in the cold, early-morning air as he waited for Farnaby and his Second, Captain Crake, to arrive. Fitzjohn showed him how to button up his coat with its 'large mother-of-pearl buttons' so that he would be less of a target – Farnaby was a crack shot. Peregrine had been practising at Manton's, but Fitzjohn was convinced that (very unethically) Farnaby was going to shoot to kill. Luckily, before shots could be exchanged, the constables arrived in a 'lumbering' coach and the two duellists are taken off to face the magistrate.

We can remember from an earlier scene in the novel that Peregrine was not a coward. He was only too ready to challenge Lord Worth to a duel when he thought that the noble gentleman had been taking advantage of his sister. Unfortunately at that point, he did not know Worth's name and when the supercilious Worth declared he would not engage with a 'country nobody', Peregrine finally declared he was Lord Worth's ward. Worth chose to keep his identity secret and merely said 'you must present my compliments to him when you see him'!

In *Friday's Child*, Westbourne Green was also the prescribed meeting place for a duel between two friends: the volatile Lord Wrotham, who never missed the opportunity for a duel, and the equally impetuous Lord Sheringham. Friends though they might have been, when Sherry found George kissing his wife Hero in an alcove at a ball he was enraged. As Georgette Heyer says, 'He ground his teeth in a very alarming manner, and rolled a fiery eye at Wrotham.' The kiss was in fact an innocent one, and as Wrotham had a reputation for both an extremely hot temper and accuracy, the Seconds decided to breach etiquette and ask for the help of the ladies in the case. When Hero approached George to beg him to apologize and not to engage with Sherry, he answered in the traditional manner by saying that he never intended to kill Sherry and would 'delope' – in other words, fire into the air. This was a permissible manoeuvre and one that allowed the parties to 'retreat' with honour. Hero was still not satisfied for, as she pointed out, what if Sherry killed George and was obliged to flee the country? George, very much amused by this, said there was no hope of Sherry killing him at a range of twenty-five yards, which was precisely why he had chosen that distance. Later in the same novel, Sherry's friends were worried that he might be tempted to call out Lord Wrotham again when he saw his wife on Wrotham's arm. Both Ferdy Fakenham and Hero pleaded with George not to accept Sherry's challenge under any circumstances as they knew Sherry was bound to be injured or killed.

Duels traditionally took place in the very early morning – light was needed, but because of their illegal nature it didn't do for many people to be about. English weather being what it is, there was often a low-lying mist at that hour, and in Sherry's case they were pleased to see it 'lifting nicely'. The duellists also provided themselves with a surgeon in case injury should occur. This gentleman would either make his own way to the site or, as in Peregrine's case, they would pick him up on the way. In order to present as little a target as possible, it was conventional for the gentlemen to dress soberly in dark clothing. Remember

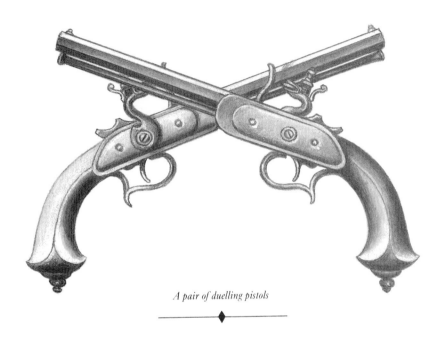

A pair of duelling pistols

how concerned Fitzjohn was about Perry's eye-catching mother-of-pearl buttons! Sherry was annoyed to see Wrotham arrive for his duel in the outfit of the Four Horse Club with its yellow- and blue-striped waistcoat with 'gleaming silver buttons'. George of course deloped and Sherry's bullet hit a tree – deliberately! The two young men, after some initial roasting, made up their quarrel and all headed off for a substantial breakfast – another more social part of the ritual.

Lord Gaywood threatened the Duke of Sale to a duel in *The Foundling* because he was so incensed that Belinda had been cleverly wrested from him. Sale, however, refused to accept his challenge as Gaywood was Harriet's brother; but also there was the question of Sale's reputation for excellent marksmanship. Sale swore that he would delope if a duel was forced upon him and Gideon tried to dissuade Gaywood from his folly with the provocative words, 'you won't hit him, you know. He is such a little fellow, and you are such a damnably bad shot!'

The threat of being called out was ever-present if one was bold enough to transgress another's rights. Sir Nugent Fotherby was worried that the Duke of Salford – the Sylvester of the novel's title – might challenge him to a duel for kidnapping his ward and nephew Edmund, and carrying him off to France in his yacht. Edmund, a delightfully precocious little boy of six years, thought it more likely that his Uncle Vester would grind up Sir Nugent's bones!

Towards the end of *April Lady* Dysart spent the drunken journey from Ryder Street to Grosvenor Square in a ramshackle hackney coach trying to call out Hethersett because he was convinced he'd seen his sister Nell coming out of Hethersett's lodging – thereby compromising herself. Dysart and his equally inebriated friend Mr Fancot were distracted by further potations and a game of dice upon their arrival at the Cardross home and a challenge was therefore avoided.

The urbane Mr Beaumaris of *Arabella* begged Mr Byng not to call him out because he was driving the mongrel Ulysses around in his curricle. 'Poodle' Byng – so called because of his predilection for being seen everywhere with a beautifully groomed poodle of pure pedigree – was convinced that Mr Beaumaris was trying to insult him. Mr Beaumaris found the situation absolutely hilarious as he himself had no choice in the matter as Ulysses wouldn't be parted from him. As he said, 'we should only make fools of ourselves, going out to Paddington in the cold dawn to exchange shots over a pair of dogs'. Mr Byng was not satisfied however until he learned that a lady was involved.

Provocation did not need to be immediate or serious, and family members were not immune to it. Although related, Vincent and Hugo were the antithesis of each other in *The Unknown Ajax* and Vincent allowed no opportunity to go by in which he could profitably needle his cousin. Lady Aurelia, Vincent's mother, voiced her husband's fears that her son might 'force a duel' upon Hugo, though neither parent could believe that their son could be so dastardly as to wish to kill Hugo. A fencing exercise between Martin and Gervase in *The Quiet Gentleman* became a serious fight when the button came off Martin's foil and he continued to fence. Unlike the onlookers Theo and Miss Morville, Gervase is convinced that it was only Martin's temper which tempted him to continue rather than an actual desire to kill his half-brother.

It is not surprising that it was unethical to challenge a man who was injured or handicapped in any way. When Venetia was caught picking blackberries on Damerel's land he took advantage of her unescorted state and ruthlessly stole a kiss from her. Instead of running away blushing she responded in her normal quick-witted way and even assured him that he had no fear of being called out for taking advantage of her as the only brother around to protect her was 'a schoolboy, and very lame'. Damerel was no stranger to duelling. When he was much younger the lady he had run away with had tired of him and gone off with a

Venetian nobleman, who surrounded himself only with black and white, including his new raven-haired, white-skinned mistress. Not only was the man extremely wealthy but he was also a superb shot and when Damerel challenged him to a duel he showed his contempt for Damerel by firing in the air, thus wounding not his body but his pride. It was the devilishly handsome Lord Wrotham, to whom duelling was second nature, who declared he would rescue Miss Milborne from that bad man Revesby and call him to account for taking advantage of her. The fact that Sir Montague was truly a man without honour was finally proved at the end of *Friday's Child* when he attacked the unarmed Mr Tarleton with his sword stick, giving him a nasty wound.

Sophy, of *The Grand Sophy*, who often acted more like a man than a woman, wanted to challenge Sir Vincent Talgarth to a duel because she felt he had stolen the Marquesa Sancia from her father. Sir Vincent happily acknowledged her skilled marksmanship and wished they had duelling pistols with them. The Marquesa intervened here, however, and said firmly that there was to be no shooting because she hated the sound of pistol shots and, more importantly, they must all get on and prepare dinner! Even the dull Lord Bromford, who had also arrived at Merton and now had his feet in a mustard bath, was moved to challenge Charles Rivenhall to a duel when Charles verbally attacked Eugenia Wraxton – rather a rash act as Mr Rivenhall owned a pair of duelling pistols and bemoaned the fact that duelling had gone 'sadly out of fashion'.

Although all the real and imagined wrongs in the novels were redressed by duelling, it was a relief to us that no serious injury, let alone death, was ever sustained, and our favourite characters were not obliged to flee the country to avoid the exigencies of the law.

CHAPTER X

BRIGHTON:
The Regent's Resort

Brighton was the most fashionable resort town in England during the Regency period, and although only a large part of one novel – *Regency Buck* – was actually set here, many of Georgette Heyer's characters repaired there at one time or another, to escape the oppressive air of London at the height of summer.

It was the Prince Regent himself, 'Prince Florizel', who had brought Brighton to such popularity. In the late eighteenth century the air and its situation had strongly attracted him and he slowly transformed the 'farmhouse' that he had bought into one of the architectural marvels of both his own age and ours – the famous Royal Pavilion.

Brighthelmstone, as it was then called, was far enough away from the stuffiness of his father's court and, with its sparkling air and fresh breezes, it provided the ideal setting for a playground of tonnish pleasures. In the Regent's wake followed the rest of society, who found much to please them in its tastefully laid out streets and gardens, its Assembly Rooms, gaming establishments and well-stocked libraries.

In Georgette Heyer's novels the Prince Regent – 'Prinny', as he was known to his intimates – was already in his early fifties. In his corpulent figure – his doctor forbade him to wear corsets on literal threat of death – there was little to remind

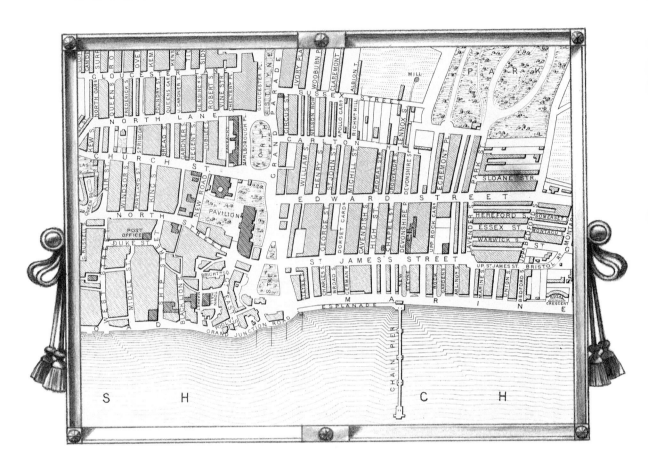

one of the handsome figure he had once been. Mrs Scattergood, Judith Taverner's chaperone in *Regency Buck*, however, 'could not be brought to see that time and self-indulgence had coarsened his features. He was the fairy-prince of her girlhood, and she would listen to nothing said in his disparagement'.

Much remains of Regency Brighton and it is certainly worth a trip there, because it is still possible to see most of the settings of *Regency Buck* and recapture the exhilaration of a sojourn in the town in its heyday.

Readers will recall only too vividly the exceptional circumstances of Miss Taverner's arrival in Brighton. Succumbing to a fit of pique against her imperious guardian Lord Worth, Judith had accepted a bet from her brother Peregrine to race down to Brighton in her own curricle. Unfortunately for her, she was overtaken by the Earl two-thirds of the way there, at Cuckfield, and her hoydenish behaviour brought home to her in no uncertain terms, 'Windblown,

The main dome of the Royal Pavilion, Brighton.

◆

dishevelled, a butt for every kind of coarse wit, an object of disgust to any person of taste and refinement!' Furious, she was forced to continue the journey by chaise and in her mortified state, entered Brighton in no mood to appreciate its glories. The next day, however, Miss Taverner's 'wretchedness' was relieved by the cheerfulness of the weather, and she was able to look forward to a 'day of interest and pleasure'.

The logical place to commence our rediscovery of Georgette Heyer's Regency Brighton is at the Royal Pavilion itself. If we approach it from the south side, we too can see that 'glistening and costly edifice' for the first time, just as Judith and Mrs Scattergood once did. Like them on their first formal visit to the Prince Regent, we enter through the Octagon Hall, where they left their shawls. Moving into the corridor, we are in what Georgette Heyer refers to as the Chinese Gallery. It was here that Judith was first introduced to the Prince and favoured with a personal tour of some of the more outstanding features of the room, including the horizontal skylight of stained glass representing Lin-Shin, the god of thunder. It was during an evening here that Mr Brummell, that arbiter of taste, excellently advised her never to admit a fault and to drive her phaeton around town to still the censorious tongues she had encountered.

Moving through the opulence of the Pavilion, we too can marvel at, if not necessarily approve of, its ornate and eclectic decor. The sumptuous red and gold of the Music Room will recall the concert that the Regent provided for the entertainment of his guests, and how the oppressive heat nearly drove Miss Taverner to the point of fainting as the 'dragons and lights started to dance oddly before her eyes'.

The fact that the Prince kept the Pavilion excessively well-heated came to Miss Taverner's aid as an excuse on a later visit. The Prince had developed a decided partiality for her and, with the promise of showing her something very pretty, beguiled her to go with him to the Yellow Drawing Room, which he called his favourite, and which she had not yet visited. The Yellow Drawing Room is now referred to as the North Drawing Room, but the decor is much as Georgette Heyer describes it in the novel, with its gold panels and plate-glass doors. Miss Taverner had no desire to be private with the Prince, but did not see how she could avoid what was tantamount to a royal command.

Having drawn her into what he referred to as the 'cosy' apartment, the Prince presented her with a snuff box and demanded to be thanked properly. He began to embrace her, and Judith committed the social solecism of fainting in his arms. The Prince's embarrassment was rendered more acute by the timely entrance of

In the North Drawing Room – the Royal Pavilion,
Brighton

◆

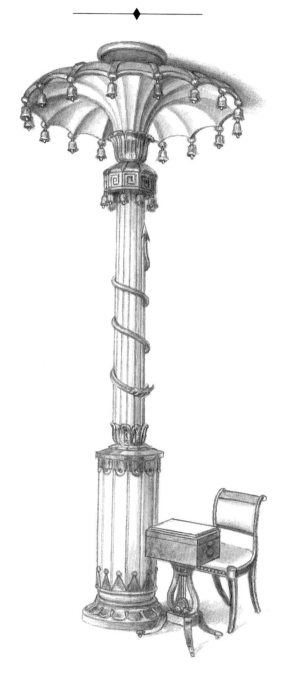

Lord Worth, Judith's guardian. It seemed as if there would be trouble between him and the Prince, but Miss Taverner was revived and, after a speaking look of relief and tenderness at Lord Worth, gathered her wits and said that the heat must have caused her to faint.

Chaperonage was an important element of society, as we can see only too frequently in the novels, and the duty of guarding the virtue of young ladies was taken very seriously. Miss Taverner, for a short while bereft of the company of Mrs Scattergood who was at the card table, was suddenly at the mercy of the Prince's advances until saved by the fortuitous arrival of her guardian.

Peregrine, Judith's brother, also had his particular invitation to the Pavilion. Unlike the ladies he was invited to dinner. According to the strict rules of society, since the Prince had no hostess it would not have been proper to invite female company to such an evening. In the Banqueting Room, we can recall how Peregrine was 'dazzled' by the rooms and 'befuddled' by the Prince's 'famous Diabolino brandy'. He gazed in constant wonderment at the largest 'lustre' he had ever seen and, viewing it like him, we too can muse on the strength of the chains that hold it up.

Before leaving the Pavilion it is worthwhile to mount the stairs and visit the rooms above – which were not open to visitors in Regency times. There you can see a hand-coloured aquatint of the original Yellow Drawing Room as it was in 1815. There is a very diverting collection of contemporary cartoons caricaturing the Prince, his life-style and the Pavilion, which lends even more colour to the various comments made about him in the novels. Also on display is a bust of the Prince Regent, and the portrait over the fireplace shows him as he was in his prime in 1787, when he was the 'young Florizel'.

Leaving the Pavilion, wind your way up past the Royal Stables to New Road. This road was built by the Prince Regent with the permission of the town commissioners, as the original thoroughfare had run too close to the western windows of his house.

Here is the theatre where Peregrine engaged a box for his sister and Mrs Scattergood, and to which outing they also invited Captain Audley, Lord Worth's more likeable brother. Though not large, they found the theatre to be comfortably set out and frequented by many of their acquaintances. The theatre has been much altered since those days and the only vestige of the original Regency architecture is the bow window at the southern end.

Turning left at the end of New Road, you will be on North Street which, until about 1780, was the northern boundary of the old town. In the time of *Regency*

The old Steyne Fountain, Brighton

◆

Buck, however, this was a 'steep, crowded highway, which was always a bustle of traffic'. So it is today, and with its modern shop fronts there is nothing to inspire us to linger.

On your right is East Street. Walking down this street, one has to ignore the ground floor and raise one's eyes up to see the original parts of the buildings. On this street Mrs Scattergood met Lady Downshire who asked her, much to her surprise, when Miss Taverner's engagement to Charles Audley was to be announced. Here, too, Peregrine encountered Mr Bernard Taverner and, feeling friendly to all the world because of his own engagement to Harriet Fairford, overcame his current 'coldness' to him and invited him to take tea with them that evening. It was also along East Street that Miss Taverner was driving when she spotted the worried Lady and Miss Fairford and discovered from them that Peregrine had not arrived to see them in Worthing.

Curving left at the bottom of East Street, we pass onto the Old Steine. This strange pear-shaped area is the focal point of Brighton. Once the estuary of the river, it is now laid out with flower beds and grassy verges. Many of the houses that were here during the Regency period can still be seen today, especially on the Eastern side. The most architecturally intact are numbers 3 and 12, but many of the others still retain their delightfully attractive original doorways. On the corner of St James Street and the Steine was the house that Lord Worth had rented and which Miss Taverner had been so keen to acquire for herself. Lord Worth had found it necessary to adopt the ploy of professing his disapproval of the house on Marine Parade in order to convince her that it was the one she should take. As soon as Peregrine saw Lord Worth's house, it was borne upon him that they had ended up with the better bargain just as Lord Worth had originally recommended.

It was to this house that Lord Worth persuaded Peregrine to return, to sign some important papers, when he met him driving to Worthing, along the Eastcliff. In its sombre interior Worth proffered Peregrine the drugged wine that Peregrine thought tasted peculiar because it was port! We were left to wonder what exactly were Lord Worth's motives as he watched Peregrine become drowsier and drowsier and finally forced the last dregs down his throat. Before leaving for the Pavilion that night, Lord Worth had the unconscious body of Peregrine bundled in a frieze cloak and carried out of his back door into a carriage. His house was one of the few that boasted its own yard and stables.

Mr Brummell also had his lodgings on the 'Steyne', but on the opposite side to Worth's. It was from there that he strolled across to visit Worth and hence was present the next day when Miss Taverner rushed in, full of anxiety that her brother had disappeared.

The Steine was also the place for the fashionable promenade at nine o'clock each evening. It was during this time that Captain Audley decided to take the air here and fell in with Mr Bernard Taverner, who was eager to discover any news of Peregrine's whereabouts. Not liking to discuss the matter in public, the Captain suggested they both go to the Castle.

The Castle stood at the north-west corner of the Steyne and Castle Square, and with the Old Ship was the leading hotel in town, until it was demolished in 1822.

While drinking at the Castle, Captain Audley, made clumsy by his lack of an arm, conveniently dropped a special marriage licence on the floor and caused Mr Taverner to hasten his own plans to marry Judith. When, under false pretences, Bernard Taverner later convinced Miss Taverner to enter his carriage, it was up the Steyne that the horses trotted, speeding their way to the London Road.

Having strolled around the Old Steine and recalled all the above scenes, remember to pause outside Steine House, now a YMCA, which is where Mrs Fitzherbert, the Prince's morganatic wife, stayed whenever she was in Brighton. Originally the house had a trellissed veranda with a balcony above, but it was entirely refaced in 1884.

Now head towards the sea and turn left onto Marine Parade. On the Parade, between Manchester Street and Charles Street, is the building which housed Donaldson's Library. Now a video store, only a discerning eye can spot the lines of the original Regency structure. Miss Taverner had been amazed 'at the spaciousness and elegance of Donaldson's'. It was to this library that, unaccompanied, she first drove her phaeton when it arrived from London, trying all the while to look braver on the outside than she felt inside.

We are never told the number of the house that the Taverners rented on Marine Parade, but we do know that it had a bow window in the drawing room on the first floor. From there Peregrine tried with his new telescope to espy bathing beauties on the beach as they left the machines and headed into the water. It must have been to this same window that Miss Taverner ran, anxious about Peregrine's disappearance every time she heard the sound of carriage wheels outside.

As you walk along Marine Parade the air is bracing. It is interesting to gaze up the side streets as you walk, for in them you will see much of the original Regency Brighton – the curved shop front in Manchester Street, the bow fronts in Charles Street, and the many elegant hooded balconies.

Carrying on along Marine Parade you will eventually come to the Royal Crescent. This is the walk on which Captain Audley took Miss Taverner to see the statue of the Regent by Rossi. Their eyes were delighted by the civilized layout of the Parade with its elegant houses, squares and crescents. The Royal Crescent is notable for the black mathematical tiles with which the houses are faced. It was in the lip of garden in the crescent that the buff-coloured statue of the Prince, made of coadeware stone, was erected. Seven-feet high, it stood on an eleven-foot pedestal. Unfortunately the stone wore badly and the arm and other portions of the statue soon broke off, leading it to be mistaken for a figure of Lord Nelson! It was finally removed in a dilapidated state in 1819.

Returning along the sea front, it is worth passing the pier to visit the Old Ship

– the oldest hotel in Brighton aside from the Castle – where balls and card assemblies were held in the Assembly Rooms attached to the hotel. These rooms are currently being refurbished, but we shall soon be able to see where Miss Taverner heard her name being 'bandied about pretty freely' after the escapade of her wild drive down to Brighton. It was at the Old Ship that Bernard Taverner, her cousin, made his passionate declaration to Judith; once again Worth appeared on the scene just as her hands were being clasped by her desperate suitor, causing Judith to blush bright red.

One last comment on the Ship before we leave it: it was here that Mr Simon, Viscount Desmond's brother in *Charity Girl*, had promised to join some friends. He wanted to go down earlier, but remembered that 'Only a greenhead would suppose that there was the smallest chance of obtaining any but the shabbiest of lodgings in Brighton at the height of the season'. As his rooms at the Ship were not reserved until the Saturday night, he was forced to remain in London.

While wandering around the streets of Brighton and taking in the resort's atmosphere, recall the other characters who had some connection with the town. Venetia's mother and father, in the novel of the same name, came here in the early months of every summer and Lord Damerel, the wealthy rake, with whom Venetia fell in love, was extravagant enough to keep his own horses on the Brighton Road to facilitate his expeditions.

The rotund Sir Bonamy in *False Colours*, whose corsets creaked but who was extremely wealthy, kept a permanent establishment in Brighton and was only seduced away from the Regent and his entertaining company at the Pavilion by his adoration of Lady Denville – Kit and Evelyn's mother. Lady Denville, not liking country life, could only bear to stay at Ravenshurst, the family home, because of its proximity to the resort. Kit, who was forced to impersonate his twin brother Evelyn to save his brother's engagement, was nearly thrown completely off-guard when an acquaintance assumed he would be in the same house on the Steyne as he had rented the year before. But it was to Brighton that Kit had to go to track down Lord Silverdale, who won the supposedly fake diamond brooch from Lady Denville at the gaming tables. The Cliffes, poorer relations and houseguests at Ravenshurst, thought Brighton far too expensive, and they elected to spend the rest of the summer at Worthing instead.

The Neaths, in *The Quiet Gentleman*, may not have been tonnish but they had money, and Mrs Neath bored St Erth as she prosed on about her projected visit to this fashionable place. The expansive Earl of Brancaster, in *Sprig Muslin*, was another frequent habitué of the town. As one of the Prince's set, he was always found at his lodging in the Steyne or at the Pavilion itself in the summer months. Georgette Heyer, however, made the point that he did not bring his wife with him on these trips, looking for female entertainment elsewhere.

For all the people in the novels who decided it imperative to spend some part of the year in Brighton, there were just as many, it seems, who decided not to do so. In *A Civil Contract*, Adam offered to take his plain little wife Jenny, the daughter of a Cit, here but she preferred to return to his family home, Fontley.

Mr Ringwood, that stalwart young gentleman of *Friday's Child*, tried to persuade Sherry to take his new wife Hero to Brighton. Lord Ringwood was convinced that she would like the Castle Inn, and being presented to the Prince Regent. However, much as Sherry wished to escape from London and the imminent arrival of his mother, he said Brighton didn't 'agree with him', and anyway they, like other unlucky characters, would not be able to procure 'tolerable lodging' that late in the season. He opted for indulging in his own pleasure, and they went to his hunting box in Leicestershire instead.

In *April Lady* Cardross had ulterior motives for proposing to take a house in Brighton. He wished to try to cure his much younger half-sister – the strong-willed Letty – of her attachment to the ineligible Allandale. His scheme was, however, thwarted at the urging of his wife, Nell. It was in this novel that a Mr Fancot, when bored with London, proclaimed the diverting words, 'There is nothing left to do here, except walk backwards to Brighton.'

Last but not least, the Ombersleys, in *The Grand Sophy*, debated whether to go to Brighton for the summer months to try and restore the poor child Amabel – who had suffered from a dreadful fever – to her former health. In the end circumstances force them, also, to remain in London, and Sophy is able to continue with her plans to remedy all the family's problems.

As we leave Brighton, gazing for a last time at its rows of shimmering houses, we should remember Miss Taverner's words in *Regency Buck*, 'Brighton passes anything I have ever seen. I wish I might stay here for ever.'

CHAPTER XI

THE SOCIETY SPA:
North-West Bath

Bath is an absolute delight for the Georgette Heyer fan for although many of the buildings have been obviously altered since the early nineteenth century, it remains more untouched than any of the other settings of her novels. Here, more than anywhere else, it is possible to gain a tremendous sense of the period. Bath, with its buildings of the famous biscuit-coloured Bath stone, is nestled in the Avon Valley, and is justifiably considered to be one of the most beautiful cities in England. Because of its reputation it has a high preponderance of tourists, and so for us – whose prime objective is to recapture the ambience of the past – it is wise to time our trip for the off-seasons or if possible, in the middle of the week.

Georgette Heyer wrote a cluster of novels set in the spa town and as there are so many interesting sights and settings to linger over it seems prudent to divide them into two easily manageable walks. The first covers the north-western part of Bath and the second, the south-eastern. Anyone pressed for time or excessively quick on his feet could manage them in one day. Otherwise they can be enjoyed at leisure.

It is constantly stressed in the novels that Bath is not the fashionable resort it once was, and that mostly elderly people lived here. Although some of the wealthy, independent heroines like Miss Annis Wychwood, Abigail Wendover and Lady Serena chose to make their home in Bath, life in the town was deemed

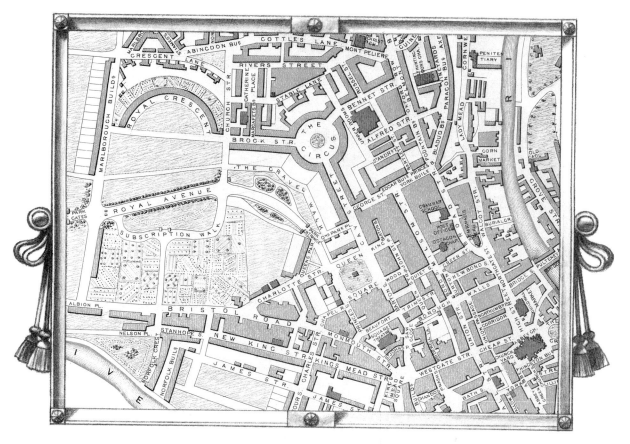

rather flat. Miles Calverleigh in *The Black Sheep* mockingly referred to everyone in Bath as being 'gay to dissipation' and couldn't wait to take Abby off to another life. Lady Serena, accustomed to greater things, was bored by the 'dawdling' pace of life in Bath – exacerbated by the oppressive summer weather. Brough, in *A Civil Contract*, is quoted describing Bath as the 'slowest place on earth'; and Lydia, during her enforced sojourn here, agreed with him. Only Sherry in *Friday's Child* disliked Bath to such a degree that he claimed he'd never 'set foot' here 'again if I live to be a hundred!'

The Duchess of Salford was treated to an exhibition of her son, Sylvester's, high-handedness when he managed to inveigle her to the hot baths completely against her will – she thought Bath was a 'horrid place'. Francis Cheviot, who decided to rest at a spa town for a while, was more ambivalent and could not decide whether he was right in preferring Cheltenham to Bath. One of Sir Bonamy's five establishments was in Bath; he resorted to the 'slightly outmoded' town purely for recuperative reasons.

Bath could also be a place for the banished. Giles Cardross threatened to send his half-sister Letty here to stay with her Aunt Honoria, who would train her to be more 'conformable'. Letty naturally thought this was a ghastly idea, 'Bath, too, of all places', and vowed that if she was forced to come here she would run away and become an actress! In *The Corinthian*, Miss Lydia Daubeney, who did nothing but cry as far as the heroine Pen was concerned, was sent to her Aunt Augusta's in Bath in an attempt to remove her from the vicinity of Piers Luttrell. Apparently, Lydia's life in Bath was all 'backgammon and spying'!

Apart from its attractions as a spa town and a place of residence, Bath was also the repository of schools or seminaries – as they were referred to – for young ladies. Cherry, the *Charity Girl* in the novel of the same name, had been abandoned at a school run by Miss Fletching in Bath and had lived here, year round, from the age of eight. Miss Fletching, whose 'Seminary for Young Ladies had been furnished neatly but austerely', was a kind woman and continued to keep Cherry long after her father had stopped paying the bills. It was to Miss Fletching that Cherry owed her appealing manners.

The headstrong and totally spoilt Miss Tiffany Wield in *The Nonesuch* was sent to Miss Climping's Seminary in Bath 'to be tamed, and transformed from a tomboy into an accomplished young lady'. Even in that august establishment, Tiffany managed to embark on a clandestine flirtation through the auspices of the day girls' society. Not everyone was unhappy in this town and as you wander around you might agree that only the most exacting person could be discontented in so beautiful a place.

Bearing in mind the differing attitudes towards Bath, start the first walk at the Theatre Royal, often referred to in the novels as the 'New Theatre', in Barton Street. Notice the plaque on the corner of the building that commemorates Beau Nash's residence. The present building was constructed in 1805 and the original main entrance was in Beauford Square, spelt Beaufort in the novels. Unfortunately the interior of the theatre was gutted by fire in 1862 and during the reconstruction the entrance was moved to its present location. If you go a little way up Barton Street and turn left into Beauford Square, you will see the original front of the theatre.

The heroine of *The Black Sheep*, Miss Abigail Wendover, known as Abby, shocked Bath society by accepting an invitation from Miles Calverleigh, the eponymous Black Sheep, to go alone with him to the theatre. Having been challenged by Miles to flout convention, she felt she could hardly say no. To compound her folly, and much to her sister Selina's horror, she also invited him

A sedan chair in Bath

to dine in Sydney Place before the play. "'Abby!" gasped Selina, turning pale with dismay. "Asked a *man* to dine with us *alone*?"' Apart from the impropriety of it, Selina would have been even more worried if she had thought that her dear Abby was attracted by this man 'with his swarthy countenance, his casual manners, and his deplorable want of address'. Abby was not in truth sure whether she did like Miles Calverleigh – he was so different from all her other suitors – but by the time Abby arrived in Beaufort Square she was ready for an evening of 'unalloyed enjoyment'. Mr Calverleigh, despite his rough and ready appearance, turns out to be an excellent host in fine romantic novel style, having hired a box and ordered tea and cakes for the interval. Throughout the evening Miles never overstepped the bounds of seemliness but treated Abby with constant solicitude. At one point, however, she was surprised, 'perceiving in his light eyes a glow there could be no mistaking'!

The theatre provided an agreeable diversion for Hero Wantage in *Friday's Child*. Having left her husband Sherry and escaped to Bath because she felt he did not and had never loved her, she was honoured to become the guest of the redoubtable Lady Saltash. Lady Saltash had much trenchant advice to offer on love and relationships. She was determined that Hero should not show a 'Friday face' but, rather, be seen enjoying herself. So she bid Hero write a note inviting two of the local, eligible bachelors to attend the theatre with them the following evening. It was at the theatre that Hero greatly amused her new admirer – Mr Tarleton – by asking him, as they walked through the foyer, if this was where the 'bits of muslin promenaded'.

One of Georgette Heyer's most diverting creations, Mrs Floore in *Bath Tangle*, actually lived in Beaufort Square, perhaps in one of the houses on the northern side of the square that have retained their Regency features. Or perhaps she lived on the eastern side where the houses are much the same as Mrs Floore would have seen them (although there the window sashes have been replaced). She was so fat that she had great difficulty getting around and couldn't bear the indignity of trying to squeeze herself into the Bath chairs. People were surprised that she had chosen to live in the Square, but she loved a 'spectacle' and pointed out that she didn't have to order out her carriage to go to the New Theatre.

As you stand in Beaufort Square recall the figure Mrs Floore must have presented with her old-fashioned purple bombazine, hooped skirts and her head nodding with vast arrays of plumed feathers. Mrs Floore had acquired her money through trade and hence was not accepted by the 'high sticklers' of Bath society; but Serena, a heroine of impeccable lineage, was drawn to her and despite the objections of her family, who considered Mrs Floore vulgar, befriended the unpretentious lady. Mrs Floore was only too aware of the class differences between Serena and herself and suggested that she should send her footman ahead to warn her of a visit in order that Mrs Floore could send her other visitors 'packing' – they would not be suitable for Serena to associate with. It was when Serena arrived in Beaufort Square on her 'good-looking mare' to take the young Emily, Mrs Floore's grand-daughter, for a ride that she discovered Emily had eloped with Gerard Monksleigh rather than marry the imperious Rotherham, who was once engaged to Serena herself.

Like Emily creeping away from her family home, we shall leave Beaufort

Gay Street, Bath

Square and turn right at the end, walking up Prince's Street to Queen Square. If one can ignore the cars, Queen Square is much as it was in Regency times. The obelisk in the centre was erected in 1738 by Beau Nash in memory of Frederick, Prince of Wales, and his consort. Although the present iron railings surrounding the square are modern, they are similar to those present in the early nineteenth century, which had replaced the original stone balustrade.

Gerard Monksleigh had made his assignation with Emily here for ten o'clock in the morning. We can imagine him waiting impatiently by the yellow-bodied carriage as Emily was, of course, late. Not having much money he could only afford a single pair of horses – to the disgust of Mrs Floore – and their

The upper end of Gay Street, Bath

consequent progress was so slow that Serena and Ned Goring were able to catch up with them and persuade them to return before it was too late.

Fanny, in *Black Sheep*, took her Italian lessons in Queen Square under the 'aegis of Miss Trimble', and Stacy Calverleigh loitered here 'interminably', hoping to see her after she failed to show up for their rendez-vous in the Sydney Gardens. It was at Miss Trimble's seminary that Fanny's friend Lavinia, at only fifteen, fell madly in love with one of the visiting professors, despite the fact that he was married and had five children. In *Friday's Child*, Sherry was convinced that Hero had taken refuge in some seminary in Queen Square because that was where 'that Bagshot woman' was going to send her. He was much put out when he discovered that Hero seemed to be having a lovely time at the home of Lady Saltash.

From the northern end of Queen Square, head up Gay Street towards the Circus. At the beginning of Gay Street don't forget to look into the window just before the door marked Number 41, where you can see an original 'powder room'. Not as steep a climb as some in Bath, the top end of Gay Street is less spoiled than the bottom end and it provides a perfect lead into the Circus which lies ahead. As you climb up the street remember that Miles Calverleigh agreed with Mrs Leavening that Gay Street 'was too steep for elderly persons'. The Registry Office in *Lady of Quality* where Miss Wychwood and Lucilla go to hire a new abigail was situated in Gay Street.

Lucilla and Miss Wychwood were on their way to the Registry Office when they ran into Ninian, who was in a hot pother. Much to Lucilla's exasperation, Ninian kept them standing about in the cold wind while he tried to explain what had made him so angry. They finally persuaded him to walk to Gay Street with them so that he could explain matters as they walked along. Once on Gay Street they parted ways. Lucilla was totally over-awed by the 'oppressive gentility' of Mrs Poppleton, who ran the Registry Office, and had to rely on Annis to handle the matter of the abigail for her. Fanny in *Bath Tangle* was awed to find herself standing beside the famous authoress Madame D'Arblay at the ribbon counter in a shop here, and was surprised to discover her buying something as ordinary as 'an ell of black sarsenet ribbon'.

The Circus, a pure round piece of road and buildings, is one of the most fascinating examples of Bath town planning. Sherry swept furiously across it in his curricle, having just seen his wife, Hero, walking on the arm of the romantically handsome George Wrotham. Sherry was on his way to Brock Street and the Royal Crescent where his mother had hired 'a palatial suite of apartments'.

Brock Street is particularly attractive with some interesting old doorways and their iron boot-scrapers. There is a stark contrast between those houses that have had their exteriors cleaned and those that haven't. The dark buildings are a tangible reminder of the length of time that the honey-colour of the Bath stone was hidden by the effects of pollution. Don't forget to look down at St Margaret's Buildings on your right with their paving stones and intriguing shops and restaurants. At the end of Brock Street the Royal Crescent fans out with a flourish. Built between 1767 and 1775 it is considered to be one of the finest achievements of urban eighteenth-century architecture and the highest point of Palladian architecture in Bath. It is as delightful to our eyes as it was to the characters of the novels. We can only admire the houses of the Royal Crescent

The corner of Brock Street from The Circus, Bath

◆

from the outside, but we are lucky in that number 1 has been restored and furnished by the Bath Preservation Trust and gives us a unique interior glimpse of how the houses in the novels might have been furnished. The furnishings in the house are actually from the end of the eighteenth century but as this was only a mere ten or fifteen years before the Regency period it is close enough for us not to quibble about.

After viewing the inside of number 1, it is exhilarating to stroll around the sweep of the Crescent and enjoy the marvellous view the houses commanded. Serena, in *Bath Tangle*, loved a good, brisk walk and didn't mind the hills in Bath at all. Out with Major Kirby, she stood in the Royal Crescent – the wind almost blowing her hat off – and echoed our own sentiments when she said, 'One can breathe up here!' She would have liked to have resided in the Crescent or elsewhere in the heights, but as no suitable house could be found to hire she had to be content with Laura Place. With the uneven paving stones underfoot, it is not difficult to half-close the eyes, banish the cars and imagine carriages and Bath chairs in their place. Head first along the green side of the Crescent until, at the end of the half-moon, the Marlborough Buildings lie opposite. This fine stretch of houses, poised on the edge of the hill, was built in about 1790 to form a

The Royal Crescent, Bath

windbreak against the prevailing westerly winds blowing across the front of the Royal Crescent. According to *The Black Sheep*, people considered Marlborough Buildings a suitable place to rent lodgings.

Turn around and walk back along the Royal Crescent on the side lined with houses. You can peer into the capacious basements which, in Regency times, would have been the provenance of the servants and the kitchens. They are now attractively renovated flats. The formerly utilitarian yards are full of window-boxes, spilling over with flowers.

Here in the Crescent the Misses Chalfont tried to flirt with Sherry, but to no avail; he could only brood about what his estranged wife Hero was getting up to in Bath. Miss Milbourne, known to the characters in *Friday's Child* as 'The Incomparable' because of her great beauty, was also staying with Lady Sheringham in the Royal Crescent, and it is from here that she set out on her ill-fated trip to Wells with Montescue Revesby – 'The Bad Man'.

Leaving the Crescent, walk back along Brock Street, turn left on the Circus, and then take the first left turn into Bennett Street. It was on this short stretch of road that Sherry, bowling into town in his curricle, 'just as the nicest precision of eye was required' saw his wife Hero walking along on the arm of Lord Wrotham. As readers of *Friday's Child* will remember, Sherry was not the most notable whip, but the ensuing accident was more disastrous than was characteristic even of him. After Sherry had extricated himself from the worst of it, he hurried after the offending pair who'd disappeared into Russell Street. We need only glimpse up this street to see which way they went before turning our attention to the New Assembly Rooms which were and are on Bennett Street, at the bottom of Russell Street.

The 'New' Assembly Rooms – so called to distinguish them from the Lower (or Harrisons) Assembly Rooms – were built between 1769 and 1771, and provided a much-needed social rendezvous and place of entertainment for the many people coming to Bath to take the waters. At the moment it is only possible to see the first octagonal hall of this fine building as the rest, the ballrooms and card rooms, are undergoing extensive repair work. It is expected that they will be re-opened in 1991.

What discreet dramas unfolded at the Assembly Rooms! The Rooms were presided over by Masters of Ceremonies, Mr King at the Upper or New Rooms and Mr Guynette at the Lower. One of the first things that visitors to Bath did was to sign their names in the subscription books. This ensured the proper attention from the Masters and, as Fanny found, 'her comfort was increased' by their goodwill. Serena, in fact, teased Fanny about the degree of solicitude she had aroused in these two gentlemen. Emily Laleham, whose spirits had not been good, was taken to the Dress Ball at the New Assembly Rooms to cheer her up. Dress Balls were held at the New Assembly Rooms on Monday, and Fancy Balls were held on Thursday. As Abby informed Miles Calverleigh in *The Black Sheep*, 'The balls begin soon after seven o'clock and end punctually at eleven. Only country dances are permitted at the dress balls, but there are in general two cotillions danced at the Friday balls.' Tea was a sixpence – this information led Mr Calverleigh, who had a very wry sense of humour, to decide that people in Bath must be 'gay to dissipation', a wonderfully ironic phrase describing the relatively staid Bath society. Miles was worried that he might be 'knocked-up by all the frisks and jollifications'. Knowing that Mr Calverleigh planned to go to the Neroli concert, Abby had, without rationalizing it to herself, decided to wear one of the new fashionable dresses she'd had made in London and to dress her hair with one loose curl hanging over her shoulder. She was definitely in 'high bloom' and in the octagon room received as many compliments as the much younger Fanny. She even had 'the doubtful felicity of being ogled by a complete stranger'! The repartée between Abby and Miles makes *The Black Sheep* one of Ms Heyer's most joyous novels. It is full of whimsically funny lines, for example when Miles described Neroli as trembling 'like a blancmange' and made the rather daring comment that the singer had 'too much of everything' – thereby causing Abby to choke on her tea.

It was at a ball in these Assembly Rooms that Miss Abigail Wendover futilely begged Miles to intervene to save her niece Fanny from a fortune hunter, his own nephew Stacy Calverleigh. Stacy, on the other hand, was relieved when he arrived at the Assembly Rooms to see that his uncle did at least possess the correct evening attire, even though he wore it in a slapdash manner. At another Dress Ball, Hero in *Friday's Child* had forgotten that she was again Miss Wantage and had moved towards the benches reserved for the use of peeresses. 'But this little slip was easily glossed over' and having been introduced to Mr King 'her social comfort was assured'.

Before leaving the New Assembly Rooms, visit the Costume Museum. There among the plethora of clothes one can see many examples of Regency dresses and can imagine our heroines wearing them in the Rooms above. Outside the Assembly Rooms, turn right twice around the building and walk down Saville Row to Alfred Street. Turn left here and then right onto Broad Street. At the busy intersection ahead you will see the famous York Hotel which, as one of the characters in the novels said, was definitely not 'dagger-cheap'. Before going inside what is now called the Royal York Hotel, stop for a moment and look at the front of the building. Originally, the hotel had three entrances, but the one on the right became the Old Post Office. Inside the hotel it is interesting to peep into the public rooms or even to stop for refreshment. Although refurbished, much of the original moulding remains. There is a 'distinguished visitor list' and some interesting prints on the wall relating to our period.

Many of Georgette Heyer's characters stayed here. In *The Foundling* the Duke of Sale's 'knowledge of Bath's hotels was naturally confined to such fashionable establishments as York House'. Ferdy Fakenham was put up at the hotel in *Friday's Child*. When, however, Sherry arrived there – seething with anger at Ferdy's role in his wife's disappearance – he was doomed to disappointment. Ferdy had sensibly made himself scarce. Ferdy could not hide forever, and on a later visit Sherry favoured him with 'a pithily worded opinion of his morals and character'. Ferdy, having received his visitor while breakfasting in bed, felt reasonably sure that he would not be physically challenged while in that refuge.

Speaking of bedrooms, none of the original rooms remain from the Regency period, though it is possible to see the room where Princess Victoria stayed while at the hotel. The best scenes set in the York Hotel are to be found in *Black Sheep*. Miles Calverleigh, despite the casualness of his clothing – he was a 'regular rough diamond' – seemed to have enough money to reside here. 'This hostelry was the most exclusive as well as the most expensive to be found in Bath; and it vaguely irritated Stacy that his ne'er-do-well uncle should be staying in it.' Mrs Leavening, Selina's friend from Bedfordshire, also planned to stay here while looking about for suitable lodgings. It was while leaving a note for Mrs Leavening that Abigail saw Miles for the first time and, upon hearing that he was called Calverleigh, made the mistake of thinking he must have been Fanny's new suitor, Stacy.

Stacy visited his uncle here and was glad of the 'small fire' burning in his private parlour. Miles Calverleigh was smoking a cheroot and was comfortably ensconced. With his total lack of familial concern he ran rings around Stacy, giving him the impression that he wasn't much more than a valet to Oliver Grayshott on the trip back from India. Stacy left in a temper and, after some contemplation, realized that the reason he was so vexed was because he had 'been made to feel small'.

Stacy's next visit to the hotel was at the behest of Miles himself, and beautifully timed to coincide with 'Mrs Clapham's' repudiation of Stacy's desperate suit. Again he was ushered into Miles's sitting-room where the table had been laid for dinner. When the brandy stage was reached, Stacy mentioned his financial embarrassment again, hoping to borrow money from his uncle. Miles, in his normal cool manner, stunned him by offering to buy the family home, Danescourt – 'sentiment', he said, 'has no place in business'. Stacy was outraged to discover that his uncle was a rich 'nabob' after all, but his desperate affairs left him no choice but to accept the terms.

Oliver Carleton, the man whose reputation was so bad that Sir Geoffrey felt

The Royal York Hotel, Bath

he was not fit company for his female relatives' society, invited Miss Wychwood, and his niece and ward Lucilla to the hotel for dinner. Miss Farlow, Annis's companion in *Lady of Quality* and one of Georgette Heyer's most famous 'gabble-mongers', was horrified by the projected engagement, also saying that Mr Carleton was not a proper person to know. Like Miles Calverleigh, Mr Carleton received his guests in a private room. The purpose of the dinner was to decide what was to be done with Lucilla, who had run away from home and been rescued by Miss Wychwood.

The Royal York Hotel was a famous coaching inn. Upon leaving, persuade the porter to take you down to the stable-yard. Here on the walls you can still see the old rings to which the horses were tied and, opening the doors to the old stables, you can marvel at how they fitted the carriages in one behind the other. Leave through the enormous old gates by which the carriages would enter and walk round to the front of the hotel again. Opposite, on George Street, are the Edgar Buildings. Here Mrs Grayshott lived in a large suite of rooms liberally provided for her by her rich bachelor brother, Mr Belling. From the Edgar Buildings, she could easily walk to the Pump Room, the shops, and the baths in Stall Street. It was Belling who was Oliver Grayshott's sponsor and who had sent him out to India. Miles was certain that this wealthy East India merchant still held Oliver in great affection and would leave his fortune to him. Oliver was 'sadly pulled' from his sojourn in foreign parts and Fanny entertained him in the Edgar Buildings with the acrostics that she had devised for him. Fanny herself admitted to spending a very enjoyable day there with her friend Lavinia and Oliver, and planned to repeat her visit.

Now turn left down Milsom Street. Today this is a thriving shopping street just as it was in the Regency period. It is an attractive road that slopes down to the lower part of Bath, and still retains much of its original character. The shops on the west side were built in the late eighteenth century.

The women in the novels ventured forth to Milsom Street for such items as silk stockings and evening gloves. Lucilla, in *Lady of Quality*, who'd lately escaped from the cloistered existence of life with her aunt, 'became rapturous when she saw the very elegant hats, mantles, and dresses displayed in Milsom Street.' With her quarterly pin-money she made several purchases, and after poring over fashion plates she ordered an evening dress and walking-habit from the *modiste* who enjoyed Miss Wychwood's custom. Milsom Street was not inexpensive, however, and like any woman Lucilla was thrilled when her new friend Corisande told her of a shop in Stall Street where she could find reticules at half the price they charged here.

In *The Unknown Ajax* Mrs Darracott and her lively daughter Anthea decided that, when they were left destitute at the death of Anthea's grandfather, they would open a mantua-maker's shop in a place like Milsom Street in Bath. They jokingly discussed whether to call it Darracotts' or Elviras', and were convinced that by charging 'exorbitant prices' they would become exclusive, and every fashionable woman would want to patronize them.

It was after she had been 'executing a commission' for Lady Saltash on Milsom Street that Hero, in *Friday's Child*, met George, Lord Wrotham, who

A Regency fanlight

with great punctilio carried her parcel for her and gave her his arm – the event which presaged Sherry's terrible crash in his curricle when he saw them together.

The exciting thought of Milsom Street's shops certainly helped draw Serena and Fanny to Bath in *Bath Tangle*. It was at one of the milliners in this street that the shockingly expensive bonnet with the green feathers reposed, which Fanny noticed had been bought by the 'odd-looking woman who dressed in such antiquated style'. Duffields, the famous library which Fanny patronized, was also on this street. These libraries, with their club-like atmosphere and comfortable lounges, were not only excellent meeting-places, but also an important link with the rest of the world. They were well stocked with 'all the new English and French publications, monthly reviews, and other magazines, all the London papers, and some of the French ones', together with the latest novels. It didn't hurt Georgette Heyer's heroines to be a little 'bookish', for it is after going to Duffields to change a book that Serena almost collided with the man she had been in love with six years before, now Major Kirkby. Both were so astonished that they end up blocking the entrance to the famous reading place as they gazed at each other in stupefaction.

Also in Milsom Street was Godwin's. Selina asked Abby to pop into that library for Mrs Porter's latest novel, but without any luck. Fanny, her niece, was pleased at the prospect of a projected trip here with her aunt, as she hated going shopping with Nurse, who said, 'The very thing one wants isn't *suitable* – as though one were still in the schoolroom!' Abby, on another visit to Milsom

Street, picked up some patterns of lace which she then submitted to the critical inspection of the sartorially wise Selina, who was still sofa-bound.

Obviously gentlemen too traversed Milsom Street, and it was here that Stacy Calverleigh encountered Miles two days after his drunken evening with him (he'd blamed his drunkenness on the quality of the brandy at the White Hart). Ever insouciant, he hoped he had not said anything untoward while in his cups, and begged Miles not to inform the Misses Wendover of his inebriated state.

Most of Georgette Heyer's heroines had exquisite taste, but the ravishingly beautiful, but simple Belinda, in *The Foundling*, was an exception. She was thrilled at the promise of a shopping expedition with Lady Harriet to the 'modish shops on Milsom Street' in the barouche, and 'visions of silken raiment floated before her eyes.' It was a purple gown in one of the shops that distracted Belinda from everything else. Unlike the demure, pastel muslin gowns that were considered suitable for young girls who were not yet out, this gown was of the brightest purple satin, 'with Spanish sleeves slashed with rows of gold beads and a demi-train, and the bosom cut by far too low!' Even the Duke of Sale was nonplussed by the gown's opulence and unsuitability. But it was obviously the way to Belinda's heart, and she even refused to run away with Lord Gaywood unless she had it. He, in a furious temper, charged off to buy it for her. When, however, she finally had to choose between Mr Mudgley, her true love, and the purple gown, Mr Mudgley won.

Keep to the right down Milsom Street and head into Burton Street. Stacy Calverleigh passed along here on his way to visit his Uncle Miles at York House. At the end, turn left and look down Parsonage Lane, which is a little further along. This is where Gerard Monksleigh of *Bath Tangle* headed off after he had exchanged some rather mendacious words with Serena and Major Kirkby, offering them a somewhat airy explanation for his presence in Bath.

Walking to the end of Upper Borough Walls, you will be once more at the Theatre Royal.

CHAPTER XII

PUMP AND CIRCUMSTANCE:
South-East Bath

Having explored the locations that are set more in the heights of Bath, we will now wander around the lower part of the town and cut across the River Avon. This was the other part of Bath in which it was also extremely fashionable to live, and it had the added advantage of being less hilly. We shall begin at the Christopher Hotel on the High Street, the other highly thought-of hotel in town aside from the York. The two hotels seem equally well respected in the novels, and often no reasons are given for choosing one over the other. The interior of this building has been drastically changed and is now a mixture of architectural styles. The coaching entrances have been blocked up and made part of the rooms, and there is very little to remind us of the Christopher Hotel our characters frequented.

In *The Foundling*, the Duke of Sale, travelling incognito, had no desire to set up at The Christopher, where he would be known. This annoyed the beautiful Belinda, his self-imposed charge, who had formed the opinion that it was 'a very genteel, elegant hotel'. But it was to The Christopher rather than to his country house that Sale decided to remove, when he cast off his disguise. Moffat, his bailiff, meets him here, and it is he who solves almost all the Duke's problems by bringing up the subject of the tenant Mudgley. Mudgley was not only one of the Duke's tenants but also, by sheer happenstance, the person with whom Belinda was deeply in love. The Duke had desperately been looking for him everywhere and it was ironic, after wandering around the country, that he should be so close to home on the Duke's five-acre farm.

The dramatic Lady Iverley, a picture of compassion and aggrieved feminine sensibility in her 'clinging robe of lavender silk, and a heavily veiled hat', put up at The Christopher when she came to Bath to rescue her son Ninian from the clutches of Ms Annis Wychwood in *Lady of Quality*. Annis, with her guinea-gold curls, had supposedly ensnared this young gentleman who was at least ten years younger than herself. It was from The Christopher that Ninian walked at 'breakneck speed' to see Annis after the meeting with his mother. His feelings had been exacerbated not only by her, but also by his sister Cordelia, who 'flung her arms' around his neck and 'wept all over' him. It would have taken a far

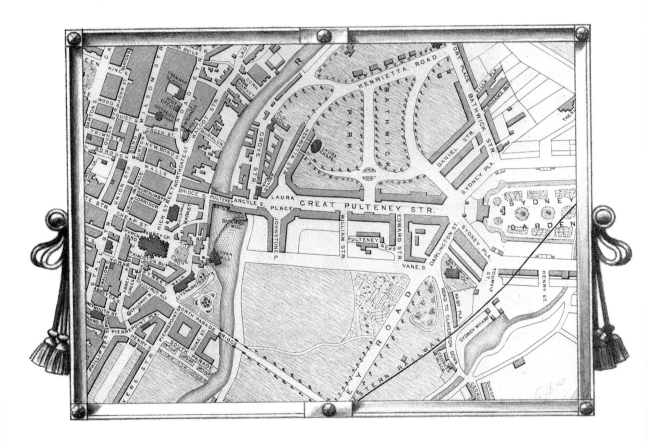

stronger man than Ninian to resist such blandishments, and he finally capitulated and agreed to return home.

Moving away from The Christopher, move on up the High Street. It was while walking along here that Mr Stacy Calverleigh, after lunching with the Wendovers in Sydney Place, made up his mind to go and visit his unknown uncle, Miles, at the York Hotel. Ahead on your right you will find Bridge Street. Having left the home of his betrothed, Harriet, in Laura Place, Adolphus, Duke of Sale, and his cousin Gideon, strolled towards Bridge Street and discussed what was to be done with the fair Belinda – the 'foundling' – whom Gideon was convinced was destined to become a 'Covent Garden nun'.

Here on this street in *Bath Tangle* Serena explained to Major Kirkby that Gerard Monksleigh, 'that young fribble', was a ward of Rotherham, who was a very bad guardian as far as she was concerned. As they walked, Serena teased the Major about his 'grave countenance'. The Major blushed slightly, guilty about his secret love for Fanny, Serena's youthful 'mama-in-law'; but he was a gentleman and was determined not to let Serena know that his heart was not completely hers any longer.

As you cross the bridge itself with its attractive shops (be sure to note number 9 Argyle Street, which has a well-preserved eighteenth-century shop front with the old fan windows at the top) you will come to Laura Place, with its interesting diamond shape. Laura Place was the major residence for Serena and the Dowager Countess Fanny in *Bath Tangle*. Their butler, Lybster, found a very 'eligible' home for them and they had signed a contract to hire it for six months.

Major Kirkby first visited them here, undeterred by the terrible rainstorm he had had to walk through. His cloak and hat were dripping wet and his hessians had to be rubbed with a leather when he arrived. Poor Major Kirkby, having been led on by Serena, expected the Dowager Countess to be a dragon and thought he had entered the wrong house when he was ushered into the drawing-room and found a youthful, frail creature sitting there with 'golden ringlets and big, soft blue eyes'! We soon discover that the Major liked his women to be helpless and delicate, and this led to many scenes with Serena who was most markedly independent and robustly healthy.

Many other differences appeared between these two re-united lovers that caused further friction. On another rainy day – remember Stacy Calverleigh said that one should never come to Bath without an umbrella – the Major arrived here in Laura Place to find Serena 'revelling in a scandalous novel'. At the time, most people did not regard novels, and especially not scandalous ones, as fit reading for young, female minds. Serena did not take kindly to his strictures, but still the Major 'was for ever in Laura Place'. Despite all their amorous complications, the two ladies were able to entertain Fanny's father so well that he resolved to stay on an extra night in Bath, being impressed with both their sherry and the excellence of Lybster.

The uncivil Rotherham was also a frequent guest on his whirlwind trips to Bath, but he, unlike the Major, was supposedly unimpressed by Serena's beauty, and told her on one occasion that she looked like a magpie in her dress of black and white.

The most amusing visit to Serena and Fanny's home in Laura Place was made by Mrs Floore. We should remember that it was Mrs Floore who was so large that she herself said she couldn't possibly travel in one of the famous Bath chairs – not only would attempting to get in one be well-nigh impossible, but the chair men would be quite overwhelmed by their burden! Fanny spotted the arrival of Mrs Floore from the window, out of which she was gazing pensively. Owing to the difference in their status, Mrs Floore had not previously called upon the ladies at home, and it was the unusual nature of her visit, as well as the fact that her carriage seemed to be tipping over with her weight, that shocked Fanny. As was the custom in these houses, the drawing-room was not at ground level, and Serena and Fanny were most sceptical of Mrs Floore's ability to ascend the stairs. Attended by the ever-faithful Mr Goring, and assisted by the support of his 'stalwart arm', Mrs Floore reached the top: only to prevent the 'lobby' Lybster – normally a model butler – from ushering her in 'like a landed salmon'. Revived by a brief respite and the ministrations of a briskly plied fan, Mrs Floore finally recovered sufficiently to be shown in to her two hostesses.

The Dowager Lady Ampleforth in *The Foundling* also resided in this prestigious location, and Lady Harriet stayed here with her. They were kind enough to relieve Sale of his bothersome charge, Belinda. The visit was not a success, however, and when Sale arrived in Laura Place a few days later, he found Harriet in an extremely agitated state, as Belinda had run away once more. Lady Ampleforth felt they were well rid of her, especially as Belinda had the misfortune to break one of her Sèvres bowls. She called Belinda 'Haymarket-ware', bringing blushes to Harriet's cheeks. When Sale later picked Harriet up here to go in search of Belinda, she found it to be the most memorable day of her life. The Duke told her that although Belinda was more beautiful, his beloved Harriet had much more countenance!

The Stinchcombes in *Lady of Quality* lived in Laura Place and Lucilla spent many a happy hour here with her friend Corisande. She was carefully escorted to the Stinchcombe residence by her new abigail, Miss Brigham, whenever Annis was not free to perform this duty herself, and she was collected by carriage at the end of the day. Even though it was now thought safe for two girls to walk together unattended by even a footman, one girl alone still had to be chaperoned. Miss Wychwood, who had taken on the responsibility of Lucilla, found this could be quite an onerous task, as she lived at the other end of town in Camden Place. Chaperoning Lucilla was especially fraught as Lucilla was extremely pretty, 'a considerable heiress' and already had several 'young men dangling after her'. Despite all Miss Wychwood's care, the disreputable Mr Kilbride still managed to intercept Lucilla and gave her his sole escort across town – an event that was likely to set all tongues in Bath wagging. In *Bath Tangle*, Serena, who was 'done with young ladyhood some years ago', felt that it was perfectly safe for her to walk about Bath by herself as it was such an 'excessively respectable town'. In London she agreed that she should probably take her maid with her or go in her carriage. Serena loved to walk – it was one of the few outlets for her high energy that were available to her in Bath. The dawdling pace of the town did not suit her, and she found her betrothed's concern for her welfare rather suffocating. Having tried futilely to persuade her to travel to his mother's in a sedan chair or a carriage, Major Kirkby at last acceded to her plan to walk up the steep hill to Lansdown Crescent – provided she accepted his escort.

Leave Laura Place now and take the walk that so many of Georgette Heyer's characters enjoyed along Great Pulteney Street to the Sydney Gardens. Trees once lined this impressive boulevard, which has otherwise remained predominately unchanged over the years. It is Bath's widest and longest street. The unspoilt house fronts and other original, remaining architectural details make it even easier to recall the flavour of the Regency. As you walk along, look at the lampholders from the eighteenth century which can still be seen in front of some of the houses, for example numbers 39, 72 and 74. These holders were known as 'throwovers'. Note also the classic six-paned Georgian sash windows and the fan-lights above the doors, especially at number 33. Great Pulteney Street sweeps up to the Sydney Gardens and to the Sydney Hotel, the building framed at the end. There is a symmetry in the streets here with the warm, honey-colour of the stone, the white doorways, the black of the iron railings and balconies, and the classical lines of the Georgian buildings. The streets are often capped by a vista of the green hills beyond, rolling round Bath.

It was while walking along Great Pulteney Street, totally immersed in her thoughts about her recent encounter with Miles Calverleigh at the York Hotel, that Abby (of *Black Sheep*) failed to see the salutation from the other side of the street of her elderly admirer Canon Pinfold. It was 'an aberration which caused the Very Reverend gentleman to subject his conscience to a severe search' to try and determine how he could possibly have offended her. Later in the novel Abby was riding down this street in a group with, among others, Stacy Calverleigh, when her niece Fanny asked her aunt if she didn't think Stacy 'as charming as he was handsome'. Abby, who had not been at all bamboozled by this iniquitous gentleman, tried carefully to intimate to Fanny that she thought him just a fortune hunter.

Major Kirkby and Lady Serena in *Bath Tangle* were so engrossed in their rediscovery of each other after six years of separation, and so busy catching up on everything that had happened to the other, that Serena failed to notice they had completely passed Laura Place and walked almost to the end of Great Pulteney Street. So absorbed were they that Serena didn't even recollect crossing the bridge!

At the end of Great Pulteney Street is Sydney Place, fanning out to the left and the right, and in front of us are the Sydney Gardens. The building straight ahead, set back from the road, is the Sydney Hotel. There are two small buildings, one on each side of the driveway to the hotel – these are the original watchman's boxes. Walk to the left along Sydney Place. In *Black Sheep*, Abigail and Selina Wendover lived in Sydney Place, together with their niece Fanny, who had not yet 'made her come-out'. It was here that Selina had her rout-party – invitations to which are highly prized. Fanny, so madly in love with Stacy Calverleigh as she was, had not however lost all sense, and she put off her plans for eloping with him until after this important event. She ended up not enjoying the party very much, being afflicted with a headache. This led to a severe case of the 'flu', which not only prevented her from honouring her clandestine meeting with Stacy in the Sydney Gardens the next day, but also effectively put an end to the possibility of elopement. In a window on this street Fanny later sat in a disconsolate frame of mind, hoping against hope that Stacy would come to visit her. It was she, therefore, who first carried the news to the rest of the household that their visitor, who had just stepped out of a hack, was Mr James Wendover – her intimidating uncle with his 'spare, soberly clad figure'.

Miles Calverleigh came to the Wendovers' house in Sydney Place to carry off his last coup. Arriving unexpectedly, and masterfully telling their butler Mitton that there was no need to announce him, he surprised Abby alone in the

Great Pulteney Street, Bath

drawing-room, where she was occupied in creating a lace collar. Caught unaware, she betrayed how much she cared for him by rushing into his arms and exclaiming that she had missed him. Having so rashly committed herself, she was then assailed by reality and forced to admit to him that they could not be married. To the amusement of the reader, Miles, who was never lost for an answer, replied in stunned *accents* 'that it is the height of impropriety to kiss any gentleman, unless you have the intention of accompanying him immediately to the altar'. Selina, who was miraculously restored to health and spirits once convinced that her dear Abby was not going to leave her and marry Mr Calverleigh, was utterly dismayed when she learned that he had had the nerve to call again. He had called at a 'most unseasonable hour' – immediately after breakfast – and Selina hurried down to break up the *tête à tête*. He casually said he had come to take Abby for a drive. Selina did everything in her power to prevent her sister going – saying it was going to rain, and that she herself wanted Abby's company. Fanny took her Aunt Abigail's side, however, and volunteered to wrap her up in 'quantities of shawls'. Off the two set in his curricle. So caught up were they in conversation, Abby was amazed to discover that they were on the London Road. Miles, with his usual aplomb, said that they were going to

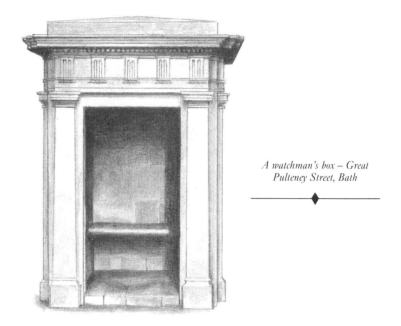

A watchman's box – Great Pulteney Street, Bath

Reading to get married, and when Abby said she would not elope with him replied, 'This isn't an elopement! I'm abducting you!' Like other Georgette Heyer heroines who left town in a hurry, Abby was finally more concerned about the fact that she didn't have a toothbrush, than about her precipitous marriage. And a toothbrush was the one thing that the well-organized Miles had forgotten to buy for her.

The last picture you should recall before leaving Sydney Place is that of the unflagging visits of the arch-intelligencer of Bath gossip, Mrs Butterbank, who could not bear not to be the first with any news. Even when a trip to the dentist meant she could not be as prompt as she would have liked, she struggled out to Sydney Place and the Wendovers, a shawl about her aching jaw, eager not to neglect her duty. It was she, of course, who was the first to inform the inhabitants of Sydney Place of Mrs Clapham's arrival in Bath. A wealthy widow, Mrs Clapham's timely *sojourn* at the White Hart had diverted the attentions of the desperate Stacy Calverleigh from Fanny Wendover. Mrs Butterbank was able to regale Selina with stories of the new couple's tea-drinking and participation in *table d'hôte* together.

On the right-hand side of Sydney Place from where you are, you will see the entrance to the Sydney Gardens. If only these gardens still had the myriad delights that they offered in the early nineteenth century! In *Bath Tangle* the

Sydney Gardens were referred to as a miniature Vauxhall, and Emily's grandmother, Mrs Floore, was determined to take Emily to the next gala night to see
the fireworks here. Gerard Monksleigh, her fledgling admirer, accompanied
them to this treat to enjoy the dancing and the illuminations. It must have been
so wonderful to see the Gardens on such an evening. Gerard managed to
persuade Mrs Floore to let him take Emily to view the waterfalls, his youthful-
ness making him seem no threat in her eyes. Gerard was impatient to get Emily
alone and learn how he could save her. With the Gardens full of two or three
thousand people, it was difficult for him to find some 'nook to appropriate'.
Emily, whose mind could really only deal with the present, did not help matters
by continually stopping to admire 'Merlin grottoes, or cascades, or festoons of
coloured lanterns'. But even if we are more 'awake' than Emily was, it must
indeed have been a sight at which to marvel.

The Sydney Gardens were not only popular in the evenings; our Bath
characters took every opportunity to stroll here on fine days. Lucilla, in *Lady of
Quality*, fell under the magic of the Gardens with 'its shady groves, its grottoes,
labyrinths and waterfalls', and she begged Miss Wychwood, her temporary
guardian, to take her to a gala night here. Miss Wychwood was dismayed to learn
that it was the charming fortune hunter Kilbride who had told Lucilla about
these delights – having artfully encountered her on her way here. Later on in
Lady of Quality, Lucilla bored everyone by constantly running to the window to
see if it had stopped raining so that Corisande's planned party could take place in
the Gardens.

In *Black Sheep*, Selina was worried that people might think her niece Fanny
was 'fast' because she was seen walking with Stacy Calverleigh in these
Gardens. It was quite improper for a young female of breeding to wander round
the Gardens – to say nothing of the labyrinth – without, of course, a chaperone.
It was while strolling in the Gardens with Serena one day, discussing her
forthcoming engagement to Lord Rotherham, that Emily, in *Bath Tangle*, burst
into tears when Serena pointed out to her that she should not be ashamed of her
grandmother – the vulgar but genuinely kind Mrs Floore. Fortuitously, Serena
was able to direct Emily into one of the Gardens' many 'arbours' and persuade
her to pull herself together. Appearances were everything, and to be seen crying
heartily in a public place was not at all the thing. They stayed secluded long
enough for all traces of the outburst to disappear, and for Serena to elucidate
that it was the Marquis of Rotherham's splendid circumstances, not his person,
that had inspired Emily with such awe and trembling.

The Gardens, as we have already seen, were a perfect place for clandestine meetings. At her Aunt Selina's rout party, Fanny, feeling pressured and ill, hurriedly agreed to meet Stacy in the Gardens the next day at two. But Fanny came down with a really bad bout of 'flu', exacerbated by the fear that Stacy would think she had stood him up. Her feverish dreams were haunted by the picture of him waiting hour after hour for her. In fact he did kill time for a while here in the Gardens but, not being a very perceptive young man, it did not occur to him that Fanny might be ill. Georgette Heyer's most shameless female character, Tiffany Wield in *The Nonesuch*, was actually squired to a fête in the Sydney Gardens one evening by a young man who pawned his watch so that they could indulge in this illicit rendez-vous – and she was still in school in Bath!

Although the illuminations and the maze have gone, the gardens are still sufficiently undulating, and landscaped in such a manner that these scenes from the past do not seem entirely improbable. We need to retrace our footsteps back over the bridge to the city centre. It is always a good idea to walk on the opposite side of the street from the one you came up on. After crossing Pulteney Bridge, take a sharp left turn on Grand Parade, which goes briefly along the river. Leaning over the balustrade you can see the water rushing through the arches of the bridge and all the old nooks in the buildings spanning the river where the pigeons have made their homes. Walk down Grand Parade until you come to the Orange Grove.

The obelisk here was erected by 'Beau' Nash in honour of a visit by the Prince of Orange. It was surrounded by a grove of trees – hence the name Orange Grove. It was not a very notable place in the novels, but the Leavenings rented lodgings here, despite the fact that it was not a very fashionable part of town. They, however, thought it a 'fine, open place' with the additional advantage that they could visit the Pump Room or go shopping without having to hire a chair. As for its proximity to the Abbey – which looms over it – and its bells, they were sure they would get used to them in no time!

Crossing the Orange Grove, a little further down Grand Parade is a plaque recording the site of Harrison's Assembly Rooms. They were unfortunately gutted by fire in 1820 – just as the Regency period ended. As Abby pointed out to Miles Calverleigh, there would be no balls or concerts at these Lower Rooms until November, but she thought he would find it an 'agreeable day promenade'. In *Friday's Child*, Mr Tarleton stood up with Hero for one of the country dances as well as the minuet here in the Lower Rooms – a gesture which amazed his friends and convinced them that he was 'in a fair way to being caught at last'.

It was at another ball at the Lower Rooms that the four star-crossed lovers of *Friday's Child* – Sherry and Hero, and George and The Incomparable – all had such an unpleasant evening. As each flirted outrageously with the wrong person to show a lack of interest, their hearts were breaking inside. The two rivals, Sherry and George, ended up leaving the ball together in absolute disgust to drink the 'very tolerable Chambertin' at the White Hart. 'So the two ladies, who had spared no pains to demonstrate their indifference to their lordships, had the doubtful pleasure of seeing them withdraw from the festivities.' After markedly ignoring each other for another hour, Hero and The Incomparable each found they had a headache and left for home.

Close by is South Parade. The enormous Mrs Floore was extremely susceptible to the heat, and caused such a stir when she collapsed in the middle of South Parade that it was as if a circus had come to town. South Parade was also where Madame Lisette, the premier *modiste* of Bath, had her 'elegant showrooms' in *Black Sheep*. She much appreciated the custom of the Misses Wendover, who were not only rich and resident, but also set off her creations to great advantage. Madame Lisette, whose real name was actually Eliza Mudford, tactfully helped Fanny Wendover decide on the style of the new outfits to be concocted from the array of silks, gauzes and muslins that Miss Abigail had bought in London. Fanny left knowing that they would 'set her in the highest kick of fashion'.

Walk past the plaque along Parade Passage by the Fernley Hotel and on your left you will find North Parade – a quiet pedestrian thoroughfare – opposite Sally Lunn's tea house, which is famous for its Bath buns and for being the oldest house in Bath. The still pristine North Parade with its flagstones once housed the Honourable Mrs Nibley, 'renowned in Bath as the town's worst archwife'. Young Lucilla, in *Lady of Quality*, had run away from home and intended to answer Mrs Nibley's advertisement in the *Morning Post* for a companion. Miss Wychwood was able to enlighten Lucilla as to Mrs Nibley's true character, and told her how all the previous companions had left in 'strong hysterics' or had been told to resign because they had not been '*sufficiently* active or willing'.

On your right off North Parade you will see a narrow little lane called Lilliput Court, which curves round and down. Pass through here and come out onto the Abbey Green with its ancient tree in the centre. Abbey Street, in the northwest corner, is where the new baths were, presided over by Dr Wilkinson. Sir Geoffrey, in *Lady of Quality*, was convinced that a course of these baths might help his wife Amabel's health, and gave that as his ostensible reason for her staying in Bath. Annis, his sister, was not deceived, and knew that Amabel was really kept there in an attempt to save her from the advances of the dangerous Oliver Carleton.

Dr Wilkinson and his baths were also mentioned in *Friday's Child*. These baths were quite private and Lady Sheringham was quite intrigued by Dr Wilkinson's plan to erect a Pump Room in Abbey Street 'where one may be able to drink four different waters'.

Go left along York Street under the arch onto Stall Street and walk along it to the right. Corisande, in *Lady of Quality*, said she knew of a shop here where you could buy reticules at half the price they charged in Milsom Street! Further down on your right is the entrance to the Pump Room – the veritable 'hub' of Bath. It is almost as exciting to visit now as it was then. Conveniently adjoining the Pump Room was the well-patronized library of Meyler and Sons, to which Fanny and the Duffields in Milsom Street subscribed, in *Bath Tangle*. Emily, in the same novel, was often permitted to go to Meyler's while her grandmama was in the Pump Room, and she suggested it to Gerard Monksleigh as a place where they could meet. He scoffed at the idea, pointing out how absurd it would be to try to have a private conversation in such a busy place. Stacy Calverleigh actually made his assignation to meet Fanny Wendover in Bath Abbey while they were both in Meyler's Library, hurriedly concocting a story that would enable Fanny to slip away without arousing suspicion. Fanny was not at all happy with the machinations and deceit that had to be employed in order for her to see him.

Today, one of the most delightful times to arrive at the Pump Room is at teatime. While consuming a refreshing cream tea and listening to the trio playing, it is easy to cast one's mind back and imagine it in Regency times. Notice the rout benches against the wall at the far end, partake of a glass of the famous Bath water, and know that you are treading in the footsteps of such Georgette Heyer's characters as: Mrs Stinchcombe, who took it for her rheumatism; Selina, for her various indeterminate ills; Fanny; the Dowager Lady Spans-borough, who disliked the taste; and Amabel, who didn't think it as horrid as she thought it might be, and certainly not as bad as the Harrogate water. The water was meant to be drunk hot, and so the brave partakers were encouraged to gulp, not sip it down.

The gossip today in the Pump Room is limited to one's own party, but the hum of conversation is as great now as it was then. The number of people present depended very much on whether it was the 'Bath Season' or not, and when the Season was in full swing there would be musicians here to entertain

A water fountain in the Pump Room Spa, Bath

the visitors. Those present in the Pump Room could be divided up into clear categories, as Georgette Heyer points out. The majority of them were 'valetudinarians' and 'dowagers', incapacitated by ill-health and age, who came to Bath and the Pump Room in the hope of a cure or alleviation of their sufferings. Then there were the residents of the town itself and the people from the surrounding countryside, for whom it was a social centre. The seasonal visitors amplified these two groups, as did their families and friends who came to attend and visit them.

It was the tradition to come to the Pump Room in the morning to take the water. But often the most important reason was because this was where one could be sure of seeing everybody. Our characters spent so much time at the Pump Room that it is difficult to choose which scenes to recall.

Lady Serena, in *Bath Tangle*, first met Mrs Floore 'of little height but astonishing girth' here. Both Serena and Fanny's attention was caught not only by this lady's size, but also because of the amazing way in which she was dressed, in an old-fashioned gown with panniers and her elaborate hats; one such hat contained 'five ostrich plumes, one bunch of grapes, two of cherries, three large roses, and two rosettes'. Serena was also bemused because Mrs Floore would sit staring at her, an incivility that was explained when Mrs Floore finally approached her and introduced herself as Emily Laleham's grandmama.

One of the most amusing sights in the Pump Room must have been Major Kirkby, who used to haunt the place every morning in the hope of seeing Lady Serena. Very much in love with his goddess, he was oblivious to the interest and amusement he was causing – one old gentleman even declared that he now set his watch by the time of the Major's arrival! Gerard Monksleigh, not knowing where Emily resided, had recourse to the Pump Room, where he finally came upon her with her grandmother after his fruitless day's search of the rest of Bath. Mrs Wychwood was able to find some young friends, the Stinchcombe girls, for her new 'ward' Lucilla here, and when Fanny in *Black Sheep* failed to keep the appointment with Stacy Calverleigh in the Sydney Gardens, he paraded around the Pump Room the next day hoping to see her. After Sherry failed to find his estranged wife Hero at home in *Friday's Child*, he had the 'happy thought' of trying to find her among the crowd in this room.

In these so civilized surroundings, it is amusing to recall Sherry's first confrontation with his estranged wife Hero. The incensed Sherry was obviously about to make a direct approach, but luckily Hero had the strong-minded Lady Saltash and her new admirer Mr Tarleton to protect her. Sherry couldn't believe it when Hero was led off in front of his nose to go dining with the presentable Mr Tarleton, but realized 'the consequences of forcing an issue in public'. Mr Tarleton, all his chivalry aroused by Sherry's 'rakish' appearance and angry mien, lost no time in obeying Hero's 'nip' on his arm and, whisking her away, felt ready to plant Lord Sheringham 'a facer' should the need arise.

Another pugilistic scene nearly occurred here in *Lady of Quality*, when the

A Rout Bench

◆

rude and egotistical Oliver Carleton interrupted a conversation between Miss Wychwood and her plodding admirer Lord Beckenham. Mr Carleton taunted his lordship with the fact that the painting he had recently paid a great deal of money for was 'dubious'. To add insult to injury, he also implied that Beckenham was a 'silly gudgeon', and finally capped it all by calling him a 'dead bore'! Through clenched teeth Lord Beckenham retorted, 'If it were not for our surroundings, I should be strongly tempted to land you a facer, sir!' Mr Carleton was saved not only by the social amenities Pump Room, but also by his superb reputation as a boxer.

As you explore the Pump Room, you will remember how, in *Black Sheep*, Miles Calverleigh asked Abby in his abrupt way to 'stroll about the room' with him, and how he amused her so much with his droll conversation and irreverent comments about people, calling, for example, Mr Dunston, one of Abby's other suitors, a 'turnip-sucker'. Abby, as we know, tried to be severe with him, but she found his comments too witty and could not help being amused. As they promenaded, Abby once again relayed to Miles her fears about Fanny's infatuation with his nephew, the 'shuffling rogue' Stacy; but Miles said he found the subject 'detestably boring' and refused to get involved.

It is not hard to imagine Serena of *Bath Tangle* being met here by Mrs Floore, who was enraptured by the letter she had received from her granddaughter

Emily describing her engagement to Lord Rotherham. 'Wreathed in smiles', she pressed Serena to read this piece of correspondence for herself. Serena, however, found Emily's account of the affair 'disquieting', as Emily filled the pages with descriptions of 'his rank, his riches, the fine houses he owned, the splendid horses he drove'. Emily rhapsodized about the number and grandness of his servants, but Serena could find no word that indicated that Emily cared personally for the man at all. Unaware of the effect of the letter on Serena, Mrs Floore was so moved at the thought of her dear Emily's happiness that she even shed a few tears of pure joy herself.

Sated with tea, music and Pump Room euphoria, head outside and, if it is raining, remember how Mr Guynette, one of the masters of ceremonies, ran out and summoned a chair for the frail and pretty Fanny in *Bath Tangle*, because 'three drops of rain had fallen'; and how Selina in *Black Sheep* was convinced that Stacy Calverleigh was a 'very pretty-behaved young man' because he too ran out of the Pump Room in the pouring rain to procure a chair for her – and in the process became absolutely drenched!

Outside the Pump Room you are in the Abbey Church Yard, and to your right is the Abbey itself. In the Regency period it still had houses butting on to it from either side, but these were demolished in 1834. The Abbey was not only a place of worship, but also – at service time – another fashionable place in which to be seen, and a decided attraction for all who had guests to entertain. It also played another role: it was a reasonably safe place in which one could meet in private, rather like the Sydney Gardens. Stacy persuaded Fanny to elope with him during a clandestine meeting in the Abbey. As chaperonage was so very strict in all other public places, and private conversation impossible at balls or concerts, other locations such as the Abbey had to be found when one was driven to desperate straits. Even in the relative seclusion available here, Fanny was horribly concerned that someone would see them together, 'If only I had a veil!' She nervously pulled her hands out of his and could hardly discuss their situation because she felt so nervous. Stacy had to use all the charm and eloquence at his command to calm her fears. Seventeen-year-old Fanny was desperately in love with Stacy, but even she had compunctions about eloping with him before her Aunt Selina's party. We, the reader, know that he was only after her fortune, and are glad to see her hold back for any reason, hoping something would happen to enlighten her to his true character. When Stacy dramatically asked how long he would have to wait before he could 'cherish and protect' her, Georgette Heyer drily commented that Abby – Fanny's other aunt

– would have thought that the only person whom Fanny needed protection from was Stacy himself.

Young Emily in *Bath Tangle* was also terrified that someone would see her slipping off by herself to the Abbey for her meeting with Gerard Monksleigh. She was not as lucky as Fanny, and found it 'overfull of visitors, wandering about it, and looking at its beauties and antiquities'. Such was her unease that she and Monksleigh were not able to make any useful plans at all.

Outside once more, head back towards Stall Street and turn right. Almost opposite you was the location of White Hart – a favourite hostelry for many of Georgette Heyer's characters on their visits to Bath. Stacy Calverleigh stayed here because he liked the bustle. This was where he encountered the bewitching Mrs Clapham, who seemed to be extremely wealthy – she had brought her own linen, and was certainly recently bereaved. On the next corner is the Round-house, an extremely interesting building architecturally and was mentioned in *The Foundling*.

Turning right again, you are now on Cheap Street, where Fanny, when 'held up by the usual press of traffic', gave Stacy a 'slight, distant bow' after his betrayal. Her coolness made him feel free to ask Mrs Clapham to marry him without any more delay. A few yards further on, you are back at the Christopher Hotel.

CHAPTER XIII

AROUND AND ABOUT:
Other Locations, Resorts and Settings

As we can see in the novels, not everyone had either the money or the inclination to visit the two most notable resort towns of Brighton and Bath. Brighton was in its heyday, and Bath already considered passé as a social venue. With Bath often being spoken about slightingly by the characters – even though some of them lived there – it is not surprising to find how disparaging they could be about the other lesser resorts.

Worthing was seen by many to be Brighton's poor relation and by others as simply unfashionable. Cressida, in *False Colours*, was obliged to accompany her grandmama there for the summer, and Kit expressed the hope that she would be so bored there 'amongst all the dowagers' that she would look more favourably upon his suit. In the same book the Cliffes discovered that Worthing possessed 'three respectable libraries' where the newspapers and magazines were delivered every morning and evening and had 'at least one very reliable doctor'! Its other great recommendation was that the charges at its comfortable boarding houses were far less than those in the more scintillating Brighton.

The young schoolboy Tom, whom Gilly rescued from his assailants in *The Foundling*, explained how he was sent to Worthing after he had the measles, adding, 'I wish it had been Brighton! That would have been something like!' On the other hand Alverstoke told Frederica that Worthing would be too expensive a place to take Felix to convalesce and suggested his country seat Alver as a more pleasant alternative. Some people to whom 'the racket of Brighton was distasteful' actually preferred Worthing. Much to Peregrine's dismay the Fairfords formed part of this number and only the thought that he might travel the thirteen miles there several times a week reconciled him to staying in Brighton.

Scarborough, high on the north-east coast had become a resort of some renown for people in the north of England. Unfortunately its benefits were soon eclipsed. As Judith Taverner said when she had made her first visit to Brighton, 'It is a thousand times better than Scarborough. And I used to think that nothing could be!' Venetia and Aubrey had never been farther from their home, Undershaw, than Scarborough. In *The Nonesuch*, another of Georgette Heyer's books set in the north, the dreadfully spoilt Tiffany Wield was nonplussed when she heard that her aunt was taking Charlotte to Bridlington for the sea air. Not one to mince her words, she labelled it 'the dullest, horridest place imaginable!' and advocated Scarborough as far superior. Josiah Steane had taken his family to Scarborough, leaving Viscount Desford to search in vain for some family connection of Cherry in town, in the novel *Charity Girl*. In *Bath Tangle*, Gerard immediately posted down from Scarborough when he learned that his guardian Rotherham had become engaged to Emily, who he thought was his own betrothed.

Harrogate, situated inland near York, had become famous for its water, and had its assembly and card rooms much like Brighton and Bath, if on a slightly smaller scale. The fullest and most amusing picture of Harrogate was given by Georgette Heyer in *Charity Girl*. In order to prepare himself for his enforced visit to Harrogate, Desford had consulted a guide which informed him that due to the town's lack of amenities it was patronized mainly by 'valetudinarians'. The town was split into two – High and Low Harrogate – and Desford was forced to traipse around all the inns and lodging-houses of both in his frustrating search for Lord Nettlecombe who, for a while, seemed to have gone completely to earth. The weather was fine, however, and despite the guide's gloomy and disparaging description of the place, Desford decided he was seeing it at its best.

Venetia was often taken by Lady Denny or Mrs Yardley to the Assemblies in Harrogate – not exactly the same as having a London season, but better than nothing at all. Once, as she told Damerel, her father even allowed her to spend a week there with her Aunt Hendred!

Lady Lindeth in *The Nonesuch* endured 'the rigours of a week spent at Harrogate' in an attempt to introduce her son Julian to the wealthy but eccentric Joseph Calver; all to no avail, however, for when he died he left his estate to

Waldo, 'the only member of my family who has paid no more heed to me than I have to him'. Miss Chartley, who lived in the vicinity, pointed out later in the novel that he probably wouldn't want to live in the Calver house as the area was so dull – even though it was quite close to Harrogate. Her friend Courtenay contemptuously replied, 'Harrogate! *That* won't fadge!'

The promise of a day out in Harrogate with Lady Colebatch and her daughter Elizabeth was enough to banish one of Tiffany's sulky moods. Tempted by such treats as visiting its premier shops, Hargrove's Library and walking down the New Promenade, she immediately went to change into one of her most dashing outfits.

Until Arabella's monumental trip to London she had only been to the assemblies in Harrogate with her mother and sister. It was to Harrogate that they went to have Arabella's wardrobe made up by Madame Dupont – an emigré from the Revolution. Later in the novel Mr Beaumaris' grandmother, the Dowager Duchess of Wigan, described Harrogate as a 'nasty, cold, shabby-genteel place, with the filthiest waters I have ever tasted in my life!'

Tunbridge Wells was another place popular with older people. Julia Oversley went to stay there with her grandmama to nurse her broken heart, away from the prying eyes of the ton in London. Not a complete recluse, her grandmama attempted to elevate Julia's spirits with 'a succession of pleasure-parties which no damsel in the possession of her senses could have failed to enjoy'. The cure was only partially successful, and after Julia fainted at the sight of Adam at Lady Nassington's party, Julia felt her only recourse was to retire permanently to Tunbridge Wells. Jenny, who was the recipient of this tragic utterance, jokingly rejoindered that 'they'd have to build another hotel in Tunbridge Wells' to accommodate all of her admirers.

In *Black Sheep* Mrs Clapham, upon meeting Stacy Calverleigh on the stairs of the White Hart in Bath, explained that she had never been to that spa before, but she had visited Tunbridge Wells. The Marquis of Alverstoke suggested to Frederica that she would find it far easier to try to launch her sister into society if she went somewhere like Tunbridge Wells, where they could attend the Assemblies rather than setting their caps at Almack's – a social citadel to which it was impossible to gain entrance without the right connections.

At the opposite end of the social spectrum Evelyn Fancot, in *False Colours*, had a 'ladybird' in Tunbridge Wells whom he occasionally visited. Unable to account for Evelyn's disappearance, his trusty servant Challow checked there for any trace of him.

Sporting Excursions

The ton of Regency England were constantly on the move, where and to whom was dictated by such ironclad institutions as the *London season*, but also by the sporting calendars which established the hunting, shooting and racing seasons.

Not surprisingly, the gentlemen in the novels were often found driving off to attend the races or other sporting events. The race tracks they visited still exist today, the most famous one in the south being Ascot. In *Frederica*, Felix's accident, and Alverstoke's desire to help Frederica with the nursing, forced the Marquis to abandon his plans to watch a horse race at Ascot, 'For the first time in many years his fellow-members of the Jockey Club would look in vain for him.' And even Harry, Frederica's older but somewhat selfish brother, decided under the circumstances to forgo the Ascot Races!

Kit, standing in for his brother Evelyn in *False Colours*, found himself constantly apologizing to his brother's male cronies for not having been at the Ascot Races. All teased him for his well-known forgetfulness, and none of them seemed to realize that they were speaking to the wrong twin. Sir Bonamy even went so far as to say that 'Evelyn' was looking better than when he'd seen him last, and thought perhaps he had been on a repairing lease.

The other most famous racing establishment was, of course, Newmarket. In *Charity Girl*, the Viscount Desford told his brother Simon that he feared he would have to miss the July Meeting at Newmarket as he suspected he would still be looking for the elusive Lord Nettlecombe. Passing on a tip he got at 'Tatts', he advised his brother to bet on a horse with the unlikely name of 'Mopsqueezer'. Later in the novel, Simon returned from Newmarket 'in excellent spirits', having enjoyed a most profitable *sojourn* there. Not only had Mopsqueezer come in first but, feeling great sympathy with his brother, Simon had then backed a long-shot called Brother Benefactor which, running at odds of ten to one, had made him very plump in the pocket. Damerel, deeply in love with Venetia but only too conscious of the disparity between his dissipated past and her innocence, nonetheless decided to stay at the Priory rather than go to the Autumn Meeting at Newmarket. Taking rather heavily to the bottle it was not a decision that his valet approved of.

Racing one's own horses was an expensive business, and Adam, in *A Civil Contract*, put his father's stables at Newmarket up for sale as an obvious economy and first step towards clearing some of the debts he had inherited. In *Frederica*, Alverstoke used the excuse of his imminent departure for Newmarket to whisk

Frederica off to see Lady Buxted without Charis's accompaniment. The same projected visit to Newmarket was also the cause of Felix's sudden arrival at Alverstoke's mansion with a demand that Alverstoke fulfil his promise and take him to see the pneumatic lift. While Alverstoke enjoyed a 'hedonistic sojourn' at the second Spring Meeting watching his filly, Firebrand, run the Merrivilles prepared for the upcoming ball.

It was while Sherry was away at Newmarket that Hero had her unfortunate gambling experience that left her so deep in debt. Sherry had not had a very successful time at the races either, due to the 'malignant behaviour of four out of five of the horses he had backed'.

Doncaster was another racing centre, and Viscount Desford knew from experience that he could post there in two days. When Dysart tried to explain to Nell Cardross how he had come by the money with which he could repay her, he cited her betting at the Doncaster Races. While staying at Castle Howard the previous year, she had apparently visited the racetrack and 'backed three winners in a row!' Dysart recouped his finances by borrowing as much as he could and putting all his money on a horse called Cockroach in the King's Plate at Chester. The predictions were right and the horse won! And in *Bath Tangle*, even the reclusive Mrs Kirkby knew exactly who Serena had been to the paddock at Doncaster with, from reading the social columns of the various journals.

Almost everybody Hero knew was horrified when they learned of her projected public race at Epsom against Lady Royston; but none more so than her husband Sherry who pointed out in no uncertain terms how unconscionable it would be, 'Epsom, of all places, with the whole world free to bet on it, and every Tom, Dick and Harry to watch it?' It was this exploit that finally convinced Sherry that there was nothing for him to do but take Hero to his mother to be taught how to behave. In *April Lady*, Epsom was also the location of the cock-fight which Dysart attended when he was meant to be escorting Nell and Letty to the masquerade in Chiswick.

Racing was so popular that even if one couldn't attend the major events it was still considered a desirable predilection. Lady Emborough, in *Charity Girl*, offered Viscount Desford 'racing at Winchester' as part of the entertainment she had lined up for him during his stay at her country house. An invitation to Badminton was much sought after during the hunting season and in *Sylvester* Lord Marlow who, 'bestriding one of his high-bred hunters . . . commanded the respect of every hunting-man', was often found there; while Serena, once her father was dead, found she dreadfully missed, among other things, her week's stay each year at Badminton. The young people in *Lady of Quality* were thrilled at the prospect of a riding-party to Badminton from Bath. As privileged 'tourists', they were treated to 'a delicious cold luncheon' put on by the Duke's housekeeper, and were shown round the house by the steward. Ninian was also excited that he was going to be able to see something of the Heythrop country which was famous for its hunting.

In *The Tolgate* Captain John Staple looked as if he were a hunting man to Sir Peter but going out with the Quorn was above his touch – as John regretfully informed him. The Quorn country required at least ten horses! Melton Mowbray, in the heart of the Leicestershire hunting country, was an area in which many a gentleman had a 'snug little hunting box'. Unfortunately Adam, in *A Civil Contract*, had to put his box up for sale, together with his late father's sixteen hunters. His man of business thought this a bad move as it would 'create a bad impression'. Adam agreed but felt he had to do it. Hero and Sherry, in their usual unorthodox fashion, spent their honeymoon at Sherry's hunting box in Melton Mowbray. Hero loved it because it was not large and imposing, or full of servants. Sherry also spent a great deal of time with her here, teaching her to ride and familiarizing her with the 'best coverts' and 'initiating her into the mysteries' of all the popular games of chance. Needless to say, they did not spend their time alone and were quickly joined first by Lord Wrotham, and then by Mr Ringwood and Mr Fakenham. As a 'bruising rider to hounds', Sherry spent a great deal of his time in Leicestershire during the hunting season, his pleasure only slightly marred by a growing concern about what Hero was up to in London.

The West

In the far west of England Bristol was a thriving port in Regency times. As such, it was predictable that Mr Chawleigh, in *A Civil Contract*, should have to go there on business. Using this excuse to further his goals, he planned to return via Bath and pick up Lydia there, in order to provide her with an escort to London. Foreseeing trouble with the Dowager Lady Lynton, Mr Chawleigh saw fit to present her with two live lobsters from Bristol which kept trying to climb out of their rush basket during his visit with the Dowager and, as Lydia said, 'He *rolled* Mama out like pastry!'

The vulgar but kind Mrs Floore in *Bath Triangle* was rumoured to be the widow of a rich merchant or ship owner from Bristol. Mr King, the master of ceremonies at the Assembly Rooms, wasn't sure which, but 'fabulously wealthy he believed'. Ned Goring worked in Bristol as a partner in her late husband's shipyard. Serena was very impressed with Mr Goring, by his easy acceptance of Mrs Floore's society, despite his superior education at Rugby and Cambridge, and by his lack of pretension in general.

Wells, about two hours' drive by carriage from Bath, was a favourite destination for a day's outing. Serena returned from one such outing totally exasperated by the 'ramshackle people' who had been allowed to join the party, the annoyances she herself had to suffer, and the ill-bred high spirits which overcame Emily and the other young members of the group.

Mr Miles Calverleigh, the Black Sheep, invited Abby to go to Wells with Fanny and Oliver Grayshott, where she intended to show him the cathedral and the famous 'mechanical device' – the clock with the knights on horseback. As the younger people wandered off by themselves, Abby was able to enjoy Miles' undiluted company, gratified that he shared her love of beauty and that their minds seemed to meet in so many ways. Oliver and Fanny quickly eschewed the cathedral and went to sit outside by the moat, where they could talk and watch the swans. Fanny partly confessed the reason for her unhappiness.

It was when the Misses Chalfont in *Friday's Child* proposed a trip to Wells to see Sherry that we saw the Viscount at his most polite. When asked if he liked cathedrals he returned the unequivocal reply 'Good God, no!' Despite Sherry's lack of interest and presence, the expedition took place, the party travelling in three carriages. It was on their return that Sir Montescue Revesby inveigled Miss Milbourne into driving back alone in his chaise by a different road and tried to abduct her.

Cheltenham, another spa town to the north of Bath, was the home of Lucilla in *Lady of Quality*. She lived under the care of her aunt, enduring what Annis calls 'the tyranny of the weak'. Her childhood friend Ninian supported Lucilla's story and told how she was almost never allowed to go anywhere alone in case she was kidnapped or the like – 'in Cheltenham, of all unlikely places' he summed up. But even in that supposedly safe town Lucilla's aunt locked all the windows and doors every night and, as an added insurance hid her jewellery under the mattress and made the butler take the silver to bed with him. Cheltenham is the town which gave its name to the phrase 'Cheltenham tragedy', which the characters in the books often accused someone of having when he or she was creating a scene or having a tantrum.

At the end of *The Reluctant Widow*, Francis Cheviot was ready to 'withdraw' from society for a while and wondered if he was right to prefer Cheltenham to Bath. Several other places west of London were mentioned in the novels. Lyme Regis was a favourite sea resort that could be visited with ease from Bath. Miss Wychwood, in *Lady of Quality*, went regularly to stay with an aunt there – proving to Mr Carleton that her world was not quite as narrow as he thought!

Marlborough, Hungerford, Newbury and Reading were all on the Bath Road and contained the important posting houses or inns where the traveller could swiftly change horses or stop and partake of refreshment. It was to Hungerford that Sylvester drove in his curricle to fetch a doctor for Tom's broken leg. Mrs Scaling, at the Blue Boar Inn, told him of a 'dangerous gravel-pit' between Newbury and Reading which was impossible to see when the snow had been falling heavily. Reading was where Tom and Phoebe hoped to get to before disaster struck and they ended up in a ditch. It was also Miles Calverleigh's planned destination when he abducted Abby in order to marry her – despite the fact that it was sixty-eight miles away from Bath!

Georgette Heyer lived for a long time in Sussex and the settings of some of her novels reflect this. *The Unknown Ajax*, for example, was set in the countryside near Rye, Hythe and Lydd. It is certainly worth making a day trip to Rye as this small historical town is completely unspoilt and one can see many of the places mentioned in the novel. A small jewel set atop a nob of a hill, Rye was once right on the sea but is now somewhat more inland. As you wander along the High Street, recall the 'dawdling' progress of Claud in his lilac pantaloons, enormous neckcloth with its large amethyst pin, and hat that 'bore a marked resemblance to a tapering chimney-pot', in *The Unknown Ajax*. The whole outfit was finished off by a cloak of Claud's own design, in 'white drab, lined with lilac silk.' Claud was obviously 'on the strut' in Rye, and Hugo rapidly became tired of his spectacular passage. Claud did show Hugo the Mint and took him up Mermaid Street to see the old coaching-house where the famous Hawkhurst Gang would congregate, 'boozing and sluicing'. After Claud's attention had been taken up by a young lady in a print dress, Hugo was left to explore the Ypres Tower by himself and was heading for the Baddyngs steps to descend to the quay when he ran into Ottershaw, the Preventive Officer. Hugo was taken on some riding trips around the local area by Richmond and Anthea and he observed how beautiful the marshland could be, and how rich it was in sheep.

Further west along the coast, Carlyon in *The Reluctant Widow* sent the new 'Mrs Cheviot' to Chichester, to 'find a tolerable silk-warehouse' where she could purchase suitable mourning clothes. Despite Elinor's usual intractability she and Miss Beccles took his advice and spent an extremely pleasant time shopping in Chichester, returning in a coach piled high with bandboxes.

To the east, Dover was the port for crossings to the Continent. In *April Lady*, one of Dysart's famous wagers was that he could journey from London to Dover and back before 'his too-hopeful challenger had made a million dots on sheet after sheet of paper'. In *Sylvester*, Lady Ingham, Phoebe and Tom were the only characters we saw stay in Dover for any length of time, and this was only due to Lady Ingham's refusal to sail unless the sea had a flat, calm surface. It was after they had been sequestered at the Ship in Dover for five days, waiting for the wind to abate and the white caps to disappear, that Phoebe and Tom discovered Sir Nugent Fotherby setting sail for France with Sylvester's nephew on board his yacht. It was in Dover that Sylvester and Phoebe had their most tumultuous scene upon their return from France. It was during the blind rage and flinging of heated recriminations that Sylvester maladroitly asked Phoebe to marry him. Further maddened by what she viewed as an added insult, it seemed nothing could heal the ever widening breach between the two of them.

Up the coast above Dover is Ramsgate. In *Sprig Muslin*, Hester Theale and Sir Gareth Ludlow discussed her planned trip to Ramsgate to help them over the awkwardness engendered by Hester turning down Sir Gareth's offer of marriage. She planned to spend part of her summer there with her brother and his wife, who were taking along their children as one of the boys was sickly and they thought the sea air might be beneficial. In *Frederica*, Felix had the 'privilege of being sea-sick' all the way from Margate to Ramsgate; despite this, the worst punishment meted out by Frederica could not mitigate the sheer joy he felt after his illicit trip on the steam-boat and his subsequent return as a stowaway. Hero was another person who committed the imprudence of going to Margate on the steam boat among the 'great unwashed'; she added that trip to her list of follies and caused Lord Sheringham, her husband, to wonder if there would ever be an end to her *faux pas*.

North of London

Heading north out of London, one of the first places mentioned in the novels was Watford, the region in which the hot air balloon with Felix on board came crashing down in the trees. Further north, Hitchin was one of the places that the Duke of Sale visited in his guise of Mr Dash – hoping to solve the problem of what to do with the foundling Belinda. In a weak moment he gave permission to the two youngsters, Belinda and Tom, to go to the fair in Hitchin while he sought out Belinda's supposed connections. Having failed in his mission, he was forced to search for the errant pair in the 'hurly-burly of the Fair'. Forgetting that as plain Mr Dash he couldn't be as 'nice' as a Duke could be, he agreed to go to the fireworks and the dancing in the evening. While Belinda and Tom were safely watching the firework display, and Sale was enjoying a few moments of peace, Sale was accosted, knocked out and then carried off by a 'neat man in a sober riding-dress'.

Huntingdon and the small villages like St Neots, in the surrounding area, featured in *Sprig Muslin*. In the novel Sir Gareth Ludlow was constantly trying to stay one step ahead of the spirited Amanda, who was innocently determined to do anything to make her grandfather give his permission for her to marry her beloved captain.

In a village close to Wisbech, Martin in *The Quiet Gentleman* was eventually picked up after his supposed abduction. Wisbech was also where Kate Malvern in *Cousin Kate* had been working as a governess until young Grittleton made her an offer against the wishes of his family who immediately turned off her. It had been the first time Kate had lived in the English countryside and she told Torquil that although the autumnal colours were lovely it rained all the time.

Lord Oversley had his country seat near Peterborough, therefore making it extremely easy for Julia to ride over to Fontley in *A Civil Contract*. Mr Chawleigh, in the same book, went on a shopping expedition to Peterborough to buy Christmas presents for all the children of the workers at Fontley. There he 'ransacked the toyshops' to such an extent that Adam said 'his memory would remain green in the district for many years to come'.

Staplewood, the Broomes' home in *Cousin Kate*, was close to Market Harborough, which was the town in which they made all their business transactions. All the letters were taken to the Post Office and this was also where Kate's new riding habit was made. It was to Market Harborough that Mr Nidd came to see how Kate was getting along, as Sarah has never received the letters that Kate sent to her. Thanks to Mr Philip Broome, Kate met Mr Nidd at the Angel. She was much impressed to see him 'looking as spruce as an onion', decked out in his Sunday best.

The great house Holkham was, of course, in Norfolk. It, like Chatsworth, was used as a yardstick by which to measure other country seats in the novels. Adam went there to learn as much as he could from Mr Thomas Coke about how to improve his farming methods and the yield of his land – as that gentleman had devoted his life to agricultural interests with tremendous success.

Journeying further north on the Great North Road, we can stop, like many of the travellers did, in Grantham. Judith Taverner, in *Regency Buck*, read Peregrine the description of Grantham in the guidebook as they travelled south on their way to London. Grantham was portrayed as being 'neat and populous' and boasting the remains of a Roman castle. All else was forgotten, however, when they arrived in the town itself and found that a prize fight was to take place nearby on the morrow and that the town was packed with sporting gentlemen. No reader will forget how significant their stay in Grantham was – the courtesy of the well-bred young man who so quietly offered up his room for their use; the friends Peregrine made at the mill; and, most of all, the cavalier fashion in which Lord Worth kissed 'Clorisande' in a lane when he found 'beauty in distress again'.

It is while Martin was safely away to Grantham, watched by Chard, that St Erth in *The Quiet Gentleman* decided the time was right to visit his cousin Theo in Evesleigh. Worried both about his wounded shoulder and the potential danger to his life, Miss Morville begged him not to go. He assured her that 'while Chard is with Martin' he stood 'in no sort of danger'. Also situated close to Grantham was Mr Beaumaris' hunting box, in which Arabella and Miss Blackburn decided to take shelter, whence her groom had gone to order another carriage so that she could continue on her journey.

York was one of the main centres of civilization in the north, and two of Georgette Heyer's novels take place in relative proximity to the city – *The Nonesuch* and *Venetia*. The characters from both books attended the Assemblies in York, and Aubrey patronized a bookstore in the town. Venetia thought he might have been there the day he failed to return home for luncheon. Until Venetia went to London she had never seen a larger town than York!

Hugo Darracott disgraced his family by marrying a 'very low, vulgar creature' who lived in Huddersfield, but their son, the young Hugo and Unknown Ajax of the title, turned out to have inherited a fortune from his parents and to own mills in Huddersfield itself. Lord Darracott was so conscious of his dignity that he could hardly bear to acknowledge 'a weaver's brat' as his own heir, and he forbade Richmond to travel up to Huddersfield with Hugo; and Hugo to even mention his connections there.

Leeds is the other industrial town, a cloth town, that featured in the novels, and it played quite a large part in *The Nonesuch*. Waldo went to York to settle all the business of the late Joseph Calver with an attorney. Readers of *The Nonesuch* will recall the eventful shopping trip to Leeds that Miss Trent made with her charge Tiffany Wield and Miss Chartley. Leeds was described in the novel as a 'thriving and rapidly expanding town' with a prerequisite amount of worthy institutions and dignified buildings of red brick that were becoming blackened by 'the smoke of industry'. Having visited the silk warehouses and other establishments, and consumed a cold lunch provided by Lord Lindeth at the King's Arms, they sallied forth once more. Just when Miss Trent was thinking what a peaceful and pleasant day it had been, the cry of 'stop thief' arose and Patience Chartley appeared in the cobbled road rescuing a young boy from under the hooves of a rearing horse. Patience's quiet bravery and Tiffany's tantrum changed the course of the book and Lord Lindeth's feelings.

Like any good novelist, Georgette Heyer wrote about the places she knew; and through the novels we can trace her own progress around the country. As we can see from the movements of her characters, people in Regency England were travelling more than ever before, assisted by better roads which were serviced by turnpikes, and well-sprung carriages – both private and public – which were newly available.

CHAPTER XIV

THE COMPLEAT TRAVELLER

L ike everything else in life, the methods of transport in Regency England depended very much on one's rank and fortune. As we have seen in previous chapters, horse-riding, for those who were both competent and able, was a favourable form of exercise, but it was also one of the simplest and most popular ways of journeying about the countryside, especially for men. Although it was perfectly acceptable for ladies to ride in the parks of London, it was not considered an appropriate means of transportation for them in town. Nor was it acceptable for ladies to drive themselves on the major public roads. As Mrs Scattergood said, it was perfectly all right to drive in the Park and 'in the country you may do as you please without occasioning remark', but she begged Judith not even to think of driving her curricle to Brighton.

Riding was especially impractical in Bath, where the 'steep cobbled streets made equestrian traffic rare'. It was far easier to walk or to hire a chair there. Miss Wychwood, in *Lady of Quality*, was irked by these restrictions, and because of them only kept her carriage horses and 'one neatish bay hack', which she could not bear to part with, in Bath. The men, however, enjoyed the freedom of riding, and often chose this form of transportation, especially on shorter journeys, instead of travelling inside a 'stuffy' closed carriage or even driving their own curricle. On the expedition down to Merton, to visit the Spanish

Sancia, for example, the poet August Fawnhope showed himself to great advantage on horseback, much to Sophy's chagrin!

In *Charity Girl*, Viscount Desford's brother, Simon, decided to ride his horse across country in an attempt to reach Inglehurst before Mr Steane could get there and confront Miss Silverdale and his daughter Cherry. Two factors were in his favour – first, he knew the countryside extremely well, and secondly, he felt that Mr Steane was not flush enough to hire a post chaise and four horses. Estimating that he would probably take the stage or the mail to the nearest town and then hire a carriage, Simon trusted that he had every chance of getting to Inglehurst first.

When Emily Latham and Gerard Monksleigh ill-conceivedly eloped together, Serena and Ned Goring volunteered to pursue them as Mrs Floore, Emily's grandmother, was too fat to travel anywhere at a realistic speed. Mr Goring was shocked when Serena suggested they chase the miscreants across country on horseback. She argued that they would be able to cover the ground far more quickly that way, and also wouldn't arouse the suspicions of the pike-keepers and other travellers on the road. Poor Mr Goring found it hard to conceive of a lady riding so far without tiring, and Serena had to remind him that she was used to hunting with the Cottesmore and thought nothing of galloping across hard country for miles!

More people than ever before were taking to travelling about the country in a wide gamut of vehicles. For those not blessed with a barouche or a landaulet in their coach-house, a gig had to suffice. This unfashionable form of transportation was not the choice of the ton, and Georgette Heyer's characters only resorted to driving gigs if such unsophisticated equipage was all they could afford. Stuck in a remote village in the countryside after the accident to the public coach, Sir Richard found that a gig was the only carriage that the landlord of the inn owned. Even then he was unwilling to lend it to a stranger, and was most impressed when Sir Richard offered to buy it from him. The Duke of Sale, who was in Baldock on his quest to find Liversedge and the public house – The Bird in Hand – rented a gig from the landlady to help him in his search. Belinda, the foundling, who had become the bane of Sale's life, was on the other hand very impressed that the man of her dreams, Mr Mudgley, drove his *own* gig!

In *Regency Buck*, the only form of transportation left for hire in Grantham on the eve of the prize fight was a shabby farmer's gig; but as Peregrine could not possibly go in his chaise, and no curricle was available, the gig it had to be. When Miss Judith Taverner first saw it (Peregrine having suggested an expedition) she said, 'I had rather walk'. Mendacious Amanda 'Smith', whom Sir Gareth discovered in a 'modest' posting house, enjoyed her ride in his curricle tremendously, for until that time the most sporting vehicle she had been in was her grandfather's gig.

The dowagers in Georgette Heyer's novels often had a predilection for travelling slowly and in state, with an entourage. So impressive was the 'cavalcade' when Sherry escorted his mother to Bath that she was given 'the most flattering degree of attention' whenever they stopped upon the road. This was not surprising, as their party consisted of 'one large travelling coach, two chaises, bearing servants and baggage, and one sporting curricle'!

Lady Lynton, Adam's mother in *A Civil Contract*, was one of Georgette Heyer's classic complainers. She travelled to London in the old-fashioned family coach and hence her journey took far longer than it normally would. Not mentioning that one of her reasons for so doing was that three people could fit into it quite comfortably, she instead berated Adam for turning away the postillions they had always kept. Mr Chawleigh, when he heard the story, was suitably depressed by the horrors of travelling in such a fashion and offered her the use of his own post-chaise and 'proper Hounslow-bred postillions'.

Her second journey was far more expeditious and impressive for she travelled post with two grooms riding with the carriage. Her retinue was completed by a coach for the servants and her trunks, and a jourgon for the furniture she wished to take with her. In *The Foundling*, the Duke of Sale, who was so cosseted that he finally ran away as plain Mr Rufford, left Sale Park for London in a style considered appropriate by his household, with 'liveried postillions, and out-riders to protect his person and his chattels from possible highwaymen'. Although he was driving his own chaise, he was naturally accompanied by another coach bearing his luggage, and preceded by all the servants thought to be 'absolutely necessary to his comfort'.

Families with children couldn't move without a fuss. Remember the number of coaches and baggage with which Sir Geoffrey and Lady Wychwood arrived in Bath for their supposed short stay. As might have been expected, Lady Denville of *False Colours* arrived at Ravenhurst in impressive style. First there appeared two coaches carrying her ladyship's servants; then a jourgon which contained 'a mountain of trunks, several housemaids, two kitchen porters, two subordinate footmen, and such articles of furniture as my lady considered indispensable for her comfort'. Finally, her ladyship made her entrance in 'an elegant private chaise'.

In contrast, the Cliffe family, who were to help make up the house-party at Ravenhurst, came in 'a somewhat antiquated travelling chariot, drawn by one pair of horses' – an equipage that Lady Denville termed 'a Gothic affair'. Arabella's uncle, the Squire, volunteered his family travelling carriage, together with his old coachman, to convey Miss Blackburn and Arabella to London. He also suggested sending one of his grooms, armed with a pistol to protect them against highwaymen. Mrs Tallant, Arabella's mother, could not remember the carriage – it'd been shut up in the coach house for so long – but the Squire assured her that it was a 'handsome' affair and not 'one of those smart, new-fangled barouches'. Sophy referred to it as 'antiquated', but her mother pointed out that a dashing 'chaise-and-four' would cost at least fifty pounds and, although the old coach was slow, it was reliable and respectable.

Lady Ingham was a capricious and difficult traveller, as Tom Orde discovered when he agreed to accompany her and Phoebe as their courier on a trip to Paris. First she decided to take her travelling carriage to Dover, then to travel post, until she realized that the three of them would have to sit 'behind', for Muker her dresser would have to have the forward seat. Much to everyone's admiration, Tom finally managed to get them all on their way.

In *The Unknown Ajax*, the vehicles in which the various characters arrived at Darracott Place provide a telling insight into their characters and status. The snobbish, 'dangerous blade' Vincent appeared driving himself 'in a curricle to which were harnessed three magnificent black geldings, random-tandem'. Only the most expert whips would drive unicorn, and the young Richmond was suitably impressed. Vincent's parents, Mr Matthew Darracott and Lady Aurelia, did not travel as fast. They came in their own 'travelling-carriage drawn by a single pair of horses', and had rested for a night on the way down. Vincent's brother, the dandy Claud, was happily driving down to Sussex in his chaise lined with pink, when his brother forced him into a ditch. The unknown quantity Hugo, who was the new heir, arrived unceremoniously, bespattered with mud, having ridden across country by himself.

In *Venetia*, Mr Hendred, who was worth at least twenty thousand a year, was a bad traveller, but could afford to travel in style and quickly – riding in his chaise with four horses and his own postillions, an equipage that much impressed the servants at Undershaw in Yorkshire when he drew up in front of the house.

Speed was everything to the whips of the ton, and horses were rated not only on their conformation and breeding, but also on how quickly they could move. Ulverston complained to St Erth that the horses which he bought from him, supposedly 'sixteen-mile-an-hour tits', in fact never achieved more than 'fifteen-and-a-half'! As we learned in *The Quiet Gentleman* when Lord Ulverston arrived at Stanyon Castle in a sporting curricle drawn by four horses, 'A curricle-and-*four* . . . is the mark of the Nonesuch' – 'someone aspiring to the highest crack of fashion'.

Miss Cherry Steane, in *Charity Girl*, was most impressed by Viscount Desford's superior curricle with its 'perfectly matched greys', as, like Amanda, the only open carriage she had previously been in was a gig. Desford had designed the curricle himself to be easy on his horses, and drove it with either a pair or a team, depending on the length of the journey. It was in his well-sprung chaise, however, that he proceeded to race around the country trying to locate Cherry's grandfather. His groom, Stebbing, was horrified when he heard that his master proposed to travel all the way to Harrogate in it. Desford believed he could complete the trip in three days, but Stebbing, who was possessed of a pessimistic turn of mind, was convinced he would be delayed by some kind of accident or the horses going lame. To allay his fears, Desford faithfully promised to stay on the post roads.

The real top-sawyers kept their own horses on the major roads. Sir Waldo, in *The Nonesuch*, teased young Lord Lindeth about travelling north by post, but Lord Lindeth knew that Waldo would definitely not enjoy being driven in a closed carriage. Nor did he think Waldo would be such a 'nip-farthing' to refuse either to send his horses ahead along the road, rent others, or accomplish the journey with one team in easy stages. The Nonesuch's arrival in the north at Brown Hall was anticipated with great curiosity by all the local young blades, but it wasn't as conspicuous as they had hoped. He entered the village in an 'ordinary perch-phaeton' rather than a curricle, and at a sober trot!

Kate Malvern's journey to Staplewood was very different from the last one she had made on the common stage. She was swept along in Lady Broome's luxurious chaise, which was 'particularly well-sprung'. Lady Broome believed in indulging in the luxury of employing her own postillions, justifying the expense because she was 'obliged to travel without male escort'. Although Miss Abigail Wendover arrived home to Bath in a hired post-chaise drawn by four horses, Georgette Heyer noted that there was nothing in her appearance 'to suggest that a private chaise, with her own postillions, would have been rather beyond her touch'. Another of her heroines, Miss Wychwood, also on her way to Bath, travelled in an 'elegant travelling carriage', but she proceeded at a very sane pace, driven by the old family coachman who refused categorically to 'put 'em

A Regency gentleman in driving gear

along' – feeling it to be grossly improper for someone of her position to travel at an unseemly speed.

Being the perfect gentleman, the Nonesuch told his newly betrothed, Miss Trent, that he would certainly not allow her to travel on the stage, but would have her collected by his own chaise and postillions. Not used to, nor expecting, such attention, the irrepressible Ancilla replied, 'Outriders, and a courier too'.

The private carriages offered great scope for personal licence in decoration and design. The fabulously wealthy Sir Nugent in the novel *Sylvester* had a special travelling coach built for his new wife Ianthe, the interior lined with blue to match her eyes. Mr Chawleigh, the wealthy Cit, in *A Civil Contract* believed in travelling in a style befitting one's rank. As a wedding gift he gave his daughter Jenny and her new husband Adam a luxurious 'posting-chariot' with the Lynton arms 'emblazoned' on it. When Jenny got her wish to go to Fontley to await the birth of their child, they departed well-prepared for their journey – two bricks under their feet and a gift of a basket of pears, some fine old Cognac, and a travelling chess-board from Mr Chawleigh.

Alice, the landlady's daughter in *Sylvester*, found that one of the luxuries provided in private chaises for winter was 'hot bricks and a fur rug'. Dolphinton also travelled in comfort in his own carriage, with the added luxury of 'a hot brick' for warming his feet and a shawl to keep off the draughts.

Hiring a private post-chaise was certainly not the most inexpensive way of travelling, but it was much less expensive than owning one. When Serena had to travel to the family home in Grosvenor Square to prepare it for the new owners after the death of her father, she went in a hired post-chaise alone (except for her maid) for the first time in her life. Previously, she had always been escorted by a courier, or had been in her father's company. Serena's Aunt Theresa was shocked that her niece should be so bold as to undertake by herself a journey in which she had sole responsibility for 'paying her own shot' at the posting house where they stopped for the evening. Not only did Serena have to assume such financial charge, she also had to undertake the hiring of the horses and postillions and order her own dinner! When one thinks of how uncomfortable it can still be for a woman travelling alone today, it is easier to sympathize with Aunt Theresa's outrage.

Gerard Monksleigh had such limited funds that when he hired a post-chaise in which to elope with Emily he could only afford one pair of horses, much to Mrs Floore's disgust. To achieve even that and still manage the rest of the journey from Wolverhampton to Gretna Green by stage or mail he not only had to sell his watch, but also his 'second-best fob and his tie-pin'. Investigating the cost of the journey, he discovered that post charges were 'one shilling and twopence per mile for each horse'.

Just as private transportation had become increasingly more sophisticated and efficient, so had the public alternatives, but no method of travelling was inexpensive, even for those who seemed relatively well heeled. Gerard Monksleigh described succinctly the expense to which he had to go in order to 'dash' across the country and visit Rotherham. First he had to take a hack to Aldersgate, then buy a ticket for the mail coach, remembering to tip the guard and the coachman; then he had to hire a post chaise and pair to take him the rest of the way. In total, the journey left him completely without funds.

When Viscount Desford in *Charity Girl* discovered that Lord Nettlecombe had gone to Harrogate, he tried to work out what could possibly have taken Nettlecombe there. The lower standard of living was a possibility, but then he balanced against that the cost of the journey north. He didn't feel that Nettlecombe could be such a 'shocking lickpenny' as to travel on the common stage, so perhaps he took the mail coach. Desford knew, however, that even *that* would not be 'dog-cheap'.

In pursuing her plan to escape from London and her aunt's scheme to marry her to her impecunious cousin, Pen, in *The Corinthian*, was determined to travel to Somerset on the stage. She scoffed at Sir Richard's suggestion of travelling post, reminding him that it would be their undoing as he was known at all the posting houses. Having settled that question, they decided to catch the coach at the White Horse Inn in Fetter Lane very early the next morning, so that the servants wouldn't see them leaving. They travelled in a green and gold Accommodation coach, and their journey was prey to the typical problems that beset Regency travellers who crossed the country in this manner.

The rules governing the coaches were strict and timetables were given out. But the time bill was often only loosely adhered to when, for example, the coachman decided he needed a drink. One of the rules the stage coachmen had to follow was not drinking while working. At the beginning of *The Reluctant Widow* we saw that this wasn't rigidly observed, as the coachman, being ahead of schedule, decided to head into the tap room of the inn for the proverbial quick drink that would not impair his driving ability. The passengers riding on top were prone to drink too much as well, and some didn't find it difficult to persuade the driver to let them 'tool' the coach for a way, to the severe alarm of the passengers inside. The combination of inexpertise and drunkenness often resulted in mishap. The schoolboy Tom, in *The Foundling*, was thrilled at the prospect of travelling on the stage. He intended to ride on the roof and make the coachman give him the reins so he could tool the coach at a gallop and, with luck, overturn it.

One of the best descriptions of the departure of a stagecoach is in *The Foundling*, when the Duke of Sale was setting forth on his life of adventure. He was amazed at all the unusual items that were being loaded into the 'Highflyer', the coach in which he was to travel, until it seemed to him that it was top-heavy and bound to overturn at the first opportunity. The yard of the inn was full of the London 'street-criers' pressing their wares on the departing passengers and offering to the Duke such seemingly useless commodities as a 'rat-trap, a bag of oranges, and a paper of pins'. The coachman, in this instance, was a real character who swore he'd never had an upset in thirty years of driving.

Delays in travel were as frequent then as they are now. Venetia, travelling by herself from London on the mail, arrived in York much later than she should have done – the coach having been 'considerably delayed by fog in and around London'. She too became very conscious of the difference in comfort between a mail coach and a private post chaise. Although she managed to book a seat, it was not a corner one and she was kept awake all night by the snoring passengers on either side of her. So little time was allowed when they stopped for breakfast that she could only drink a sip of coffee before they were off again.

How quickly the ground could be covered was a matter of great pride when such valuable horseflesh was involved. Roads were being improved all the time, and in *Regency Buck* the virtues of the new road to Brighton over the old were extolled. As Georgette Heyer said, 'Twenty-eight stagecoaches a day ran between London and Brighton during the season', taking approximately six hours to complete the journey. A light travelling chaise would take about five hours, and Peregrine hoped to do it in about four and a half hours in his curricle. Bernard Taverner and his father, having travelled post, arrived in Brighton at the Castle Inn at four o'clock, the journey having taken just less than six hours from Piccadilly.

Unlike the mail coaches, the Accommodation coaches were not known for their speed. It would be highly unlikely for them to cover more than an average of eight miles an hour. Sir Richard took this salient fact into account when he worked out how to overtake Pen, who had run away convinced that he'd only offered for her because he thought he had to. Borrowing the Honourable Cedric's bays, and driving a light curricle, he felt – quite rightly as it proved –

that he would be able to intercept the coach around Chippenham. We are given an evocative word-picture of it as it hoved into Sir Richard's sight. Georgette Heyer described it as a 'green and gold monstrosity', top-heavy with passengers on the roof, the baggage cramming the boot, and the guard, with his yard of tin, seated at the back.

Miss Malvern was forced to travel on the stage back to London from Wisbech when she was turned away from her job as governess in the novel *Cousin Kate*. Despite her experience of the world, she still found the journey a trial – 'six of us inside!' – and like other travellers she had no time for more than a few sips of coffee when they stopped. Kate was vexed with herself for being so 'ticklish', but her old nurse was shocked to find her precious charge had found it necessary to travel on a 'common stage'. Ninian Elmore rescued Lucilla from having to venture on the stagecoach, calling her an ignorant schoolgirl because she didn't know that one had to be on the waybill in order to get a seat.

Having persuaded Mr Calver to drive her into Leeds, Tiffany Wield's plan to run away to London on one of the coaches suffered a major setback. Never having travelled by herself before, Tiffany had no idea what times the mail and the stage left, nor how to get a seat. Mr Calver was going to have to be coaxed into providing even more help. When Courtenay and Miss Trent discovered Tiffany had gone, Courtenay scoffed at the idea of Tiffany 'condescending to a stage-coach! A post-chaise-and-four is what she'd demand!' But Miss Trent knew that Tiffany didn't have sufficient pin-money left to afford that kind of expense, as it would have cost at least £25.

Travelling in any form of transportation was extremely fatiguing, and some found it hard to bear even relatively short journeys with physical equanimity. When Fanny and Serena moved to Bath from their house in the country, they only had to journey about twenty-five miles, which they accomplished in a barouche. They were in such an optimistic frame of mind at leaving the confines of Milverley, that although Fanny had to be 'fortified on the road by smelling-salts', she said she'd never had a more comfortable journey. Instead of arriving with a sick headache in Bath and retiring to bed, she was able to 'inspect' their new house and stay up for dinner to discuss the latest news – the engagement of the Princess Charlotte to Leopold of Saxe-Coburg.

In *Venetia* Mr Hendred was an extremely bad traveller. Even the shortest distance brought on his tic, and he executed each journey as quickly as possible. For example when he journeyed down to London with Venetia, he wished to spend only one night on the road. Not only did Mr Hendred's tic come on, but he also found it impossible to eat after he had been travelling. Venetia knew how to alleviate his ill, exhausted state and had pastilles burnt in his room and a tisane prepared for him when he retired to bed.

When Gervase Trent, the Seventh Earl of St Erth, returned to his ancestral home to claim his inheritance, his welcome was not a warm one; in fact, several members of his family resented the fact that he had survived the war. His autocratic stepmother, who was used to holding undisputed sway at Stanyon Castle, suggested that he retire early after the rigours of his journey, despite the fact that it was only fifty miles and he had travelled in a 'luxurious chaise'.

Even the healthy, young Viscount Desford was exhausted after travelling for two long days in his post-chaise. It was so lightly built and well sprung that it could travel quickly, but it also 'bounded over the inequalities of the road', which made it impossible for him to sleep in it. So bored was the Viscount that he made the shocking disclosure that he wished he could take the place of one of the post-boys! Upon reflection, however, he decided that he would not enjoy wearing the prerequisite leg-iron.

Many characters of the novels suffered from travel sickness. Little Tom, the child with the offending tooth in *Lady of Quality*, couldn't go for even a mile without feeling nauseous, and his family constantly had to stop the coach to accommodate him. The precocious Edmund, Sylvester's nephew, was another poor traveller; he turned 'queasy every time he goes in a chaise', as Sir Nugent discovered to his horror. Edmund certainly spoiled the first part of their honeymoon trip by 'waking up and crying, and saying he wanted to be sick'. When returning to London from Dover later in the novel, Sylvester deliberately provided a phaeton as well as a chaise so that Edmund could travel in an open carriage in which he was apparently never sick.

In *Sprig Muslin*, Amanda played a naughty trick on the old, fat Mr Theale, who was convinced she would be his new lovebird. Amanda, whose determination to marry her soldier was matched only by her innocence, began to realize that Mr Theale's intentions were not very honourable, and evolved the brilliant idea of convincing him that all the raspberries and cream she had consumed, together with the motion of his carriage, had had disastrous effects. A bad traveller himself, Mr Theale was not only gullible but also extremely sympathetic when Amanda launched into her charade.

Even the romantically inclined were not free from such mundane considerations. When Emily and Gerard eloped in *Bath Tangle*, Gerard had the horse 'sprung' in order to avoid pursuit. They started to travel so quickly that Emily began to feel sick and, despite their fear, they had to slow down. The sensible Mr Tarleton, in *Friday's Child*, went so far as to abduct Hero by tossing her into a post-chaise, but he was not foolish enough to try to make love to her in a carriage 'nicknamed, not without good reason, a bounder'.

The various equipages used for travel in Regency England did not always run smoothly, and accidents were a common occurrence. The most irritating were those caused by the reins being taken by young blades who wished to demonstrate their prowess with the ribbons. This happened frequently on the public coaches, and as the new 'driver' usually tried to go too quickly these escapades often ended in disaster, to the distress of the other passengers. We can see a classic example of this in *The Corinthian*, when Pen and Sir Richard were travelling inside the Accommodation coach. As its speed increased, and the passengers became only too aware of what was happening, their panic grew. Taking a bend too tightly the coach ended up on its side, the windows smashed and its occupants tossed upon each other. Not only was the coach seriously damaged, but in this case 'one of the wheelers had badly strained a tendon'.

Arabella, in the novel of the same name, was initially beguiled by the novelty of her journey to London – the passing sights and the posting houses' accommodation. After a while, however, the unwieldy progress of the Squire's old coach became rather irksome, as the journey was dragged out by delays like reshoeing the horses instead of being able to have a new pair put-to. The groom didn't even have the traditional and very necessary 'yard of tin' to warn the pike of their approach. The antiquated coach almost made it as far as Grantham, but the perch broke and 'the body fell forward upon the box. The Squire's travelling carriage has stood too long in his coach-house.' Stranded on the roadside, the air wet with rain and dusk upon them, Arabella determined to seek shelter and headed for the lights she saw off among the trees. Here she encountered one of the most wealthy, famous and heart-hardened members of the ton – Mr Beaumaris.

Viscount Desford's return journey from Harrogate was unhappily not as trouble-free as the journey up. First he lost a tyre and then 'one of his wheelers went dead lame', so that the journey took five days instead of three. Knowing that he couldn't allow Phoebe to run away to London on the common stage, and that it would be not only financially impossible but also not good ton for her to travel there post, Tom, her childhood friend, volunteered to take her himself. He announced he would drive her all the way, having borrowed his father's curricle pulled by 'two tidy brown steppers, Trusty and True'. All went well, despite the heavy snow, until a donkey and cart appeared on the road.

What with the donkey braying at Trusty, who hated them, and Tom catching his heel in the coach rug, they ended up in the ditch with a broken shaft and smashed near-side wheels. True had sustained a sprained left hock and Tom a broken leg. The broken leg was the least of Phoebe and Tom's worries – they were more concerned about the horse and the damage to his father's curricle!

Perches were obviously a heavily stressed component of the carriage's build, as that was the part that frequently gave way. Mr Theale, having 'lost' Amanda, was going on his way, happily anticipating arriving at his hunting-box 'when Fate intervened', as Georgette Heyer said, and the perch of his carriage broke. Luckily Mr Theale was not hurt, and the only discomfort he suffered was having to walk a mile to the nearest small posting-house where he comforted himself in front of the fire with a bottle of brandy and the ordering of a choice meal.

Travelling in Regency England could be fraught with danger – highwaymen, the criminals of the road, were an ever-present threat. No journey could be undertaken with the surety of reaching one's destination still in possession of one's valuables. We have already seen the precautions that travellers took to protect themselves from highwaymen – the guard on the box and the outriders who rode alongside the carriages. Since at that time London proper ended at Hyde Park Corner, even a drive to Kensington could entail laying oneself open to attack.

On the night that Nell and Letty were forced to go to the masquerade in Chiswick by themselves because Dysart, their escort, had stood them up, they did not even think of taking outriders. Despite the passage of time and the encroachment of the developers, it is not difficult to imagine their coach slipping in the 'bright moonlight' through all the places we are so familiar with – Kensington, Hammersmith, and on to Chiswick Mall. A sudden pistol-shot pulled the coach up sharply, and it is interesting that it was the bold Letty who was the more terrified of the two, begging Nell to 'give them everything'. This particular hold-up had a surprising end, however, and neither the jewels nor the lives of the two ladies were really threatened.

A far more sinister attack took place in *Regency Buck*, when Peregrine was driving himself back from the Fairfords in Hertfordshire, where he had been making a prolonged stay. He was driving across Finchley Common by Turpin's Oak – now completely smothered by suburbia – when he was fired upon by a lone horseman standing in some trees. His new groom Hickson – the one who

A Regency highwayman

---

did not know how to sound the yard of tin – acted quickly and thrust Peregrine out of his seat so that the bullet missed. To the amazement of Peregrine, Hickson then drew out his own pistol and fired – without success – upon the stranger. Perry shrugged off the attack, but Judith and Miss Scattergood were much more alarmed, especially as this was the second dangerous situation Peregrine had recently been in.

In *The Foundling* a great fuss was made when it was thought that Tom, the schoolboy whom Sale had befriended, had held up a stagecoach and been subsequently put in jail. Apparently Tom had told the coach in question to 'stand and deliver' in the appropriate manner and then let off a shot which singed the coachman's ear. Sale was loath to believe that Tom was so wicked, and after much interrogation of the various parties he discovered that the 'pop' had not been caused by gunshot but by a ginger-beer bottle! Tom, like the Duke himself when he was younger, considered highwaymen like Dick Turpin to be romantic figures, and not in the same immoral class as other thieves. Stealing was not really stealing when a highwayman did it!

Another 'mock' hold-up which wasn't meant to be serious, but rapidly became so, took place in *Sprig Muslin*. The young Hildebrand was of a romantic disposition to begin with and, when confronted by the beautiful Amanda and her tale of abduction, all his chivalry was fired and he agreed to help her escape from Sir Gareth by holding them up and carrying her away on his horse. Suitably dressed for the part in a mask and 'voluminous cloak', all went well until Hildebrand's horse started to play up and inopportunely shoved into him while he was trying to keep Sir Gareth and the post boy covered. The pistol went off and Sir Gareth suffered an almost fatal shot in his left shoulder. It was only Amanda's presence of mind and swift, pragmatic action that prevented Sir Gareth from bleeding to death. Here, too, they had a lot of explaining to do to prove that Hildebrand was not a hardened criminal.

The famous Brandon diamonds were stolen – supposedly by highwaymen – in *The Corinthian*. In classic fashion Lady Saar's travelling coach had been stopped by two masked men with pistols. The surprising element in the whole story was that the highwaymen knew where to look for the necklace which was not in the jewellery case but in its secret hiding-place behind one of the red silk squabs. Rose, Nell Stornaway's former nurse in *The Tollgate*, was actually in love with a highwayman. She met him when he held up Nell and her, and dealt with him in such a peremptory manner that he immediately apologized for being so bold as to stop them. He also provided them with the magic password 'the music's paid' should they ever be confronted by a highwayman again. Rose's Mr Chirk was a most unusual highwayman – far superior to most – who wanted to make enough money to buy a small farm and give up the 'bridle-lay'.

Lady Lade, one of the most notable female whips of the time and the only person to rival Miss Taverner's skill with the ribbons, had actually been the mistress of a highwayman called 'Sixteen-String Jack' before her marriage made her somewhat more respectable. When Sophy, in *The Grand Sophy*, had to explain at Merton why Lord Charlbury's arm was in a sling, she quickly invented a tale of highwaymen who held them up on the road. In the 'flurry of shots' – nothing serious, of course – Charlbury was hit despite his immense bravery. Such nobility on Charlbury's part was more than enough to re-activate Cecilia's love. Another of Georgette Heyer's heroines, Arabella, became so tired with the tedium of her journey to London that she almost wished to be accosted by highwaymen.

Just as there was a clear-cut hierarchy in the types of vehicles one could have seen on the roads in Regency England, so also was there that same hierarchy in the houses that served them – from the elegant posting houses to the common inns. In *Regency Buck* we were given a description of the two great rival posting houses in Barnet – the Red Lion, which catered for the northbound vehicles, and the Green Man for those going south. Apparently competition between the two was so fierce that they had been known to intercept forcibly private chaises and change their horses. Sir Peregrine and Judith enjoyed the free refreshments handed to them – a glass of sherry and sandwiches – one of the advantages of the Green Man.

In *The Tollgate*, Captain John Staple took upon himself the temporary job of gatekeeper at one of the turnpikes. He admitted that he found the work exasperating as he could never be far from the gate for any length of time. He was also bemused by the number of people who tried to cheat on the tolls.

As we have seen, Georgette Heyer's characters were happy to speed their way around England and, with the exception of the threat of highway robbery, the problems they encountered were not much different from those of our own time.

A cast iron bollard adapted from a cannon

◆

CONCLUSION

◆

After this exploration of Georgette Heyer's world the perceptive reader will constantly come across more tangible details of the period and be reminded of other incidents in the novels that have not been covered here. The architectural graciousness can be seen in odd nooks and crannies all over England and with it the vibrant presence of her characters, driving along the country lanes, pulling up at elegant houses, following the hunt, and even in such mundane preoccupations as blackberrying. The geographic limitations have been set by the areas that were important during the Regency period: London, the spa towns and the country houses which spread across the land from north to south. But there is another reason for the proscribed locations; like all good writers Georgette Heyer only wrote about those places she herself knew well.

In order to assist the reader who may have missed some of the novels a list of those referred to in this book has been appended. The keen reader will also probably want to read the other novels she wrote which were set in the latter part of the eighteenth century, but they do not have their place in this work. It is the Regency period which Georgette Heyer made peculiarly her own.

Many of the strictures that ruled the lives of her heroines and heroes of the ton still exist today and provide the ultimate guide to good manners. So if we find ourselves unconsciously emulating their speech and becoming more decorous we have only retreated to a more 'proper' world whose mores are not lost to us even today.

LIST OF NOVELS REFERRED TO IN THE BOOK

Regency Buck

The Grand Sophy

Friday's Child

Venetia

Sylvester

Bath Tangle

Cotillion

Arabella

Lady of Quality

The Nonesuch

False Colours

A Civil Contract

Charity Girl

Cousin Kate

Black Sheep

April Lady

Sprig Muslin

Frederica

The Toll-Gate

The Quiet Gentleman

The Foundling

The Reluctant Widow

The Corinthian

The Unknown Ajax